RACING
REFLECTIONS

The Lives and Times of Irish Racing People

MARGARET LANTRY & JANE O'KEEFFE

SUPPORTED BY HORSE RACING IRELAND

Irish Life and Lore
Recordings and Books

HORSE RACING
IRELAND

First published in 2012
Irish Life and Lore
Ballyroe
Tralee
Co. Kerry

www.irishlifeandlore.com

ISBN 978-0-9574611-0-9

This publication has received support from Horse Racing Ireland.

Typeset in Ireland by Swerve Design, Dublin.
Printed and bound in the EU.

CONTENTS

Introduction

Each, capall, larach – these are some of the words used in the Irish language over centuries to describe horses; *marcach* is the Modern Irish word for 'horseman' or 'jockey'. Several academic works have focussed on the words for 'horse' in Celtic languages. The eleventh-century *Lebor na gCeart* (The Book of Rights) even has a phrase *"eich luatha re lecon"*, which means "horses that are fast away" (Book 1, page 1454).

This selection of profiles of trainers, jockeys, bookmakers, breeders and others working in jobs related to the thoroughbred horse industry illustrates the Irish love of horses continuing to this day. Whether it is in creating the stableyard environment that best suits the horse on a day-to-day level, treating the horse in a humane manner, or creating the best showcase at racecourses, the lives of these people show their determination and passion to allow the horses to come to their full potential. These are lives lived with purpose and resolve. The men and women featured in this book reflect on long lives lived in the realm of horse racing in Ireland. Running throughout the recorded voices is a link which connects each one with the other, and that link can best be described as a wholehearted and genuine love of horses.

Here are the personal voices of owners, trainers, jockeys, stewards, racecourse managers and craftsmen, as they recall their childhood days and those who influenced them in early adulthood. In these pages are described the world of horse racing in Ireland in earlier days and races won and lost. Famous bloodlines, the transport of horses by train, the original facilities at racecourses, the immense changes which have come about for good or ill, controversies, triumphs and failures are all described. Stories about the varying personalities of owners and trainers, not to mention the unique personalities of individual horses, are also included.

These biographical essays are based on interviews carried out by Maurice O'Keeffe of Irish Life and Lore and the quotations used in the text of the book are taken directly from these recorded interviews. Maurice has travelled the length and breadth of this island listening to people's histories, and these people have generously responded by inviting him into their homes and their lives. The photographs which illustrate this volume are all personally chosen by them. Whilst it has been wonderful to bring together the recollections of people, the photographs bring back memories, especially of horses, such as Arkle, Mill House, Teapot and many others. Unfortunately, due to the passage of time, it has not always been possible to name each person or all locations in the photographs so any information about these would be gratefully received on www.irishlifeandlore.com or info@irishlifeandlore.com. These profiles are based on original interviews, all available online.

When listening to these interviews, it is striking how much these people credit good fortune in their lives. They work long and hard hours every day but they know that when it comes to the time to show their horse in the arena – whether in a race or show – other factors beyond their control come into play. All workers deal with 'unknown unknowns' (as was infamously said by Donald Rumsfeld) but these people have to deal with more than most – the weather, infection, injuries, the track – and these are just outside the yard. Yet everyday trainers and yard staff are up very early day in day out to go through the same routine in order to keep the animals under their protection in the best condition. Even after a big win at the races, trainers must return to the daily grind as Jacqueline O'Brien tells us in her profile. The jockeys ride the same tracks over and over. Mick Kinane is asked whether this becomes boring – only, he says, if the race is not going well!

It is a commonplace to write of the sport of racing, but to these business people this is far from just being a sport. This is a serious business. Some people talk about the issue of increasing prize money in order to attract owners, as without owners there is no business. Looking after race horses is very expensive; the jackpot can be huge but so are the losses. Again Mick Kinane talks about the joy of winning for owners, and he notes that it is the same whether for a millionaire or a shopkeeper. The reason for this joy brings us back to our theme – the real love of horses.

Mentioned in these pages are some great horses, such as Arkle, Mill House, Sea The Stars and Golden Miller, known to true aficionados of the sport, but other fondly remembered horses are also here, such as The Bower, Teapot and Fort Leney. Early Irish winners such as The Liberator, trained at Mounthawk in Tralee, which won the 1879 Galway Plate and The Wild Man from Borneo, owned by the Widgers of Waterford, which won the 1895 Grand National are also recalled. Although the success of the Irish has been immense within the past half-century, this has its origins in much earlier times.

Some of the memories and stories recounted in this book stretch further back in time than others. When deciding on the order of contents, it was felt that a chronological approach would be best, and would be more enjoyable for the reader. Great achievements do not come about by accident. Beginning with such trainers as Tom Dreaper, who used interval training and brought Arkle to winning form, and Vincent O'Brien, who examined every facet of a horse's life and surroundings and looked at every detail ensuring that everything under his control would be done to perfection. O'Brien developed his own gallops and walked them every day, as Tommy Murphy tells us; he played music to the horses so that they would get accustomed to noise, ferried the horses in a Skyvan so that they would arrive in a fresh condition, and made sure that the horses were perfectly turned out on race day. This attention to detail by several trainers over decades has ensured that the expert training of horses in Ireland is now recognised worldwide. This is a sector of the economy that provides support to tens of thousands of employees, self-employed jockeys, feed merchants, construction, equipment sales, racecourses, bookmakers, bloodstock agents, and so on. Forming the foundation of the industry are the owners and trainers. The support of owners, the success of trainers and, most importantly, great horses are the three pillars on which the industry is based.

With this selection of profiles of people in the horse racing industry, their hard work and dedication is saluted. Their lives and times were comparatively more difficult than today, but still they carried on, working hard in the belief that they were engaged in valuable labour – which it certainly was – as can be seen by their great successes.

Margaret Lantry and Jane O'Keeffe

Foreword

How often do we have cause to regret that the people in our lives did not commit their life's memories to paper or at least tell their story to someone who could carry the memories to share with others? Very few have the time or opportunity to write it all down and so, little by little, whole histories may be forgotten. It was that thought which led to the commissioning, for the Horse Racing Ireland archive, of an aural record of 'the lives and times' of a broad selection of people who have been at the heart of the story of Irish racing for many years.

The greatest pleasure to be experienced in Irish Racing is to be in the company of extraordinary people with a great passion for horses and horse racing. We are rightly proud of our country's reputation as the nursery for some of the best thoroughbreds in the world, ideally suited by landscape and climate to producing horses blessed with speed, stamina and endurance, but above all it is the people, with their native talent and understanding of the horse, who make the real difference.

Irish Life and Lore has collated the stories of forty-six people who were, and are, at the heart of the living history of the sport in Ireland. They have been saved in a set of CD recordings which will be lodged in the HRI archive, at Ballymany on the Curragh, and made available online. The people involved told their tales to Maurice O'Keeffe with an openness and generosity that truly franks the form, as our racing writers might say. Each one brings a different perspective on the world of Irish racing and leaves a legacy for the future. It is a very different type of racing history, going well beyond the records of the racing calendar to bring us into the homes, stable yards and racecourses where the daily human dramas were lived out.

This book has been written around a selection from the recorded archive, with the contributions chosen to give a vivid picture from as many different viewpoints as possible. *Racing Reflections*, and the audio archive behind it, mean that the lives and times of the men and women who built the foundations of what is now one of Ireland's most successful and respected industries will always be there to inspire and inform future generations. It is because of them and the many others like them, whose stories remain to be told, that Ireland is universally seen as one of the best places in the world in which to breed, train, race and buy and sell thoroughbred horses.

Denis Brosnan

Denis Brosnan
Chairman
Horse Racing Ireland

Acknowledgements

Without the gracious co-operation and generosity of the people featured in this book, this work would never have seen the light of day. From the initial contact by Maurice O'Keeffe of Irish Life and Lore, right through the process of the compilation of each recording and the provision of personal photographs and memorabilia at the final stage, each and every person was an absolute pleasure to deal with.

The Irish Life and Lore Horse Racing Ireland Audio Collection was commissioned by Horse Racing Ireland as a service to the Irish racing industry and to form part of the Irish Racing archive.

We are particularly grateful to Denis Brosnan, Chairman of Horse Racing Ireland, for his most interesting and informative Foreword. Mr Brosnan has spent 21 years at the helm of Irish racing, guiding it though the many authorities including Bord na gCapall, the Racing Board and the Irish Horse Racing Authority.

We would like to thank Michael O'Rourke, Tamso Doyle and Martin Murphy at Horse Racing Ireland for their support and great attention to detail.

Brigid O'Hea has done sterling work in the proofreading of the various drafts, and her fine work deserves acknowledgement. Thanks also to Colin Hanley at Swerve Design and to Spectrum Print Logistics.

Caroline Norris, Peter Mooney and The Irish Field were of enormous assistance in the provision of old photographs, for which we are very grateful. We also thank Ann Whelan of The Turf Club for providing photographs. Where the source of a photograph is known, it is acknowledged in the caption.

This book is based on interviews recorded by Maurice O'Keeffe. Audio recordings were mastered expertly, as always, by sound engineer Barra Vernon, Cork.

Margaret Lantry is a qualified librarian and experienced researcher. She is a freelance consultant who provides research, computer, and publishing services to public and private institutions and individuals. She is currently researching the history of an Irish landed estate.

Jane O'Keeffe is an author of several books including *Recollections of 1916 and its aftermath: echoes from history* (2005) and *Chronicles of Cork: an oral record* (2010). Her latest publication *Voices from Great Houses – Cork and Kerry* will be published by Mercier Press in 2013. She works in partnership with her husband Maurice O'Keeffe in Irish Life and Lore.

Marguerite winning the Open Ladies race at the Naas Harriers Point to Point on Capparoe in Two Mile House on March 8 1944.

CHAPTER 1

MARGUERITE WELD

" The night before Clonmel show, we stabled the horses at Powerstown. Then, you rode one horse and led the other the two miles to Clonmel. "

PROFILE

Marguerite Weld

Springbank
The Curragh
Co. Kildare

Born:
1915

Occupation:
Trainer and
breeder

arguerite Weld of Springbank on the Curragh is now in her 97th year. She is a wonderful lady, full of stories of her childhood, her family and, naturally, of horses.

As a child she had difficulty saying her full name, and when 'Gita' emerged, the name stuck, and she became widely known as Gita. It is not a diminutive she cares for, so she will be given her full name here.

Marguerite Connolly, one of a family of three girls and one boy, comes from near Kilsheelan, close to the border with County Waterford. Her father was a dairy farmer who worked an old property, and her mother was Alexandra O'Mahony from 'The Wilderness' near Clonmel. Alexandra's bachelor uncle Alexander lived at Powerstown Park which was sold after his death to Villiers Morton Jackson, after which it became the Clonmel Racecourse.

Encounters during the Civil War

When Marguerite was about 7 or 8 years old during the Civil War, a farm labourer took refuge in their kitchen one day where her mother and a servant named Maggie Landers, were working. Marguerite, who was upstairs playing in the nursery, looked out the window and saw a man running across the stableyard towards the house.

The man was ragged, dirty and unkempt. At first, the family did not recognise him but when he begged for food and for help, they saw it was Ned Davin, who had once worked on the farm. Marguerite, at the nursery window, saw a gang of men wearing trenchcoats running towards the house. As recounted to her later, the armed men stormed into the kitchen and demanded that the man, whom they described as their prisoner, be given up. Maggie Landers was terrified but started reddening the poker in the fire! At the barrel of a gun, Marguerite's mother pleaded that Ned be first allowed to eat, which was agreed, and then the prisoner was manhandled out the door. From the window above, Marguerite saw the group leaving, and shortly afterwards she heard several shots being fired. When she went down to the kitchen her mother had collapsed with the shock and had to be put to bed. The following day, Marguerite asked Johnny Roche, a farm labourer, about the shots she heard, and he told her that Gilda, their Kerry Blue dog had been shot at. It later became clear to her that Ned Davin had been executed that day.

Some time afterwards the IRA demanded a billet for about thirty men at the farm. Marguerite's mother refused to let them sleep in the house with the children. However, across the yard stood an empty oats loft accessed by an outside stone stairs where the men were allowed to sleep, though the situation was abhorrent to the Connolly family. The men would drill outside, and although the children were kept away from them, Marguerite remembers watching the drilling. The brigade supplied food which had to be cooked and served by the Connollys. Marguerite recalls that there were about six officers (one of whom had gone to Trinity College Dublin), who insisted on being served their meals in the family dining-room, but at the insistence of Mrs Connolly, their guns were left in the hall. Naturally, the family were in constant terror of being burned out by the Free State army, in reprisal for housing the IRA.

Working with horses

Marguerite's love of horses was engendered quite early in her life. Her father ran a dairy farm, but also bred and trained horses including Comeragh Bill and Comeragh Lass. Marguerite ascribes her love of horses, and her knowledge, to her father. Her step-uncle, Willie O'Mahony, of 'The Wilderness', Clonmel, rode as an amateur, but tragically, following a head injury from a fall, he died from meningitis.

Marguerite has a photograph of herself on horseback at the age of three. Apparently her mother was dismayed when the young Marguerite threw aside her dolls and other girlish delights in favour of a wooden pull-along horse on wheels! As a child, Marguerite delighted in going to any horse-related event and in those days during the 1920s and 1930s, cars were not common. Travel was either on horseback or by pony and trap. The Connollys at that time walked a puppy for the Waterford Hounds, of which George Waterford was Master. Marguerite's first outing with the Waterford Hounds was at the age of 10, which, was also the last occasion on which her father hunted. Her mount was a great big grey hunter with a gentle nature. The Waterford Hounds went out with the Clonmel Harriers, whose Master was Mick MacCarthy who ran a great pack. Marguerite remembers him as a great Master but quite cross, so the children were terrified of him. Sometimes, she stayed with the MacCarthys at Gortnafleur in Clonmel, helping with the breaking in of horses..

Marguerite was sent to boarding school at the Ursuline Convent in Waterford which did not suit her at all as she had no contact with horses. During the holidays she went showjumping to various shows including Clonmel, Cork and Piltown, and she rode Right Ho, a bay, at the RDS. Her father was delighted with her success, but her mother was not quite so impressed!

As Marguerite points out, travel to the shows was not as straightforward as it is today with the horsebox hitched to the SUV. Back then there were no horseboxes, and Marguerite would travel the day before the show. At Clonmel, she would stable the horses at Powerstown Park, stay with the MacCarthys at Gortnafleur and then compete the next day, riding home that evening. It was common to ride one horse to the event while leading another. Usually Marguerite rode to events alone, as her sister had no interest in horses and her brother had left home to stay with an aunt in Dublin while attending secondary school there.

To work on a horse during the War

After school, Marguerite worked with the Department of Agriculture, based in Naas. Just before the Second World War broke out, she had an ex-thoroughbred Capparoe sent from home, which she stabled in Hanlon's yard and fed with hay bought from local farmers. Petrol was rationed, and bicycles were commonly used for work. However, Marguerite requested permission from her boss to use her horse for travelling to the hilly parts of Wicklow. He brought the matter to a committee, and it was decided that she be allowed to ride the horse for work purposes. Marguerite was delighted as the horse was being exercised, and she then also brought him to point to point events.

On one occasion during the war, and in the midst of a rail strike, when she needed to get the horse home for the Easter holidays, she rode home in stages from Naas to Carlow, from there to Kilkenny and onwards to home. Even though this worked out well Marguerite recalls that she could only bring the bare minimum of luggage on horseback with her!

During the war years, she regularly won point to point races with the Naas Harriers on Capparoe. She remembers the events as being quite competitive, and other eventers included Eileen Wright (née Buckley) from Dublin. The usual race was three miles over mixed jumps and open country, which included ploughed fields which were pretty bad in wet weather.

Training horses

It was during this time that Marguerite met Charles (Charlie) Weld at a meet with the Kildare Hounds. After their marriage, they moved to England and when Charlie took out a licence as a trainer, they trained horses for about two years for Dr Pashgar, an Indian doctor.

After a few years, Charlie became unwell and they returned home. They moved to Dunsinea, at the Phoenix Park, in the 1950s and continued training there. Others training there at this time included Willie Byrne and Maxwell Arnott. Some of the owners the Welds worked with were Bertie Kerr, Desmond Butler (a stockbroker in Dublin), Dr Pashgar and Alistair Billing. The McGraths and the Brabazons were some of the other trainers at the time. The Welds were very successful but this success required more space, so they had to rent stables from other yards, including Hendrons, for the overflow. It was not so much that the Welds were getting the top horses, but they were looking after them well, Marguerite explains.

There were very good people in the yard, she remembers, including Charlie Newman, their headman, who was excellent. He lived in Cabra with his parents who were both elderly and ill, and when the Welds moved to Kildare, he had to remain in Dublin to look after them. Marguerite recalls that people were more anxious for work in those days, as jobs were scarce.

The move to the Curragh

The time came when the Welds needed a larger property to sustain their business. The property at Rosewell on the Curragh, previously owned by the jockey Morny Wing, had been empty for some time and was now up for sale.

There were no horseboxes at this time, and private transport was not available. However, there was a railway siding at the Curragh, so Marguerite made an arrangement with CIÉ to move twenty horses. On the appointed day, they rode the horses through the Phoenix Park to the station there and after the journey by rail, they rode to the stableyard at the other end. This was done in two runs with the help of Marguerite's brother and Peter MacCarthy.

> 66 There was a rail strike. I set off from Naas with the horse and rode him to Carlow, the next night to Kilkenny and then home to Kilsheelan. 99

The option was given to the staff in Dublin to work at Rosewell, but not all of them wanted to move to County Kildare. Some did travel, but many returned again because they missed the bright lights. Marguerite interviewed many new people, including Joe Malone who was employed at Rosewell as a young man, and who later became headman for her son, Dermot.

Once they moved to the Curragh, Charlie Weld was consistently on the list of the top four trainers. As Marguerite points out, with a smaller number of trainers at the Phoenix Park it was hard to provide good facilities for exercising the horses. Undoubtedly, the good gallops at the Curragh played a part in this success as the horses could be exercised there.

Success

Both Marguerite and Charlie were involved in training. Due to Charlie's illness at the time, Marguerite was caught up with the work at the yard as well. From an early age, their son Dermot was also keen on horses. Marguerite remembers bringing him to a sale in England one winter during the school term. He was attending Newbridge College as a day boy, and as there was no-one to look after him overnight in her absence he was given permission to accompany her. The sale was at Newmarket, and with the filly, they travelled over on the boat. At the sale,

Charlie Weld being led in by his brother John and wife Marguerite after winning a race at the Two Mile House Point to Point (mid-1940s), his friend Ned Coffey is on the other side.

Roll of Honour, bred by Marguerite Weld, winning the 1970 Grand Prix de Paris.

Frank Pagano, Mary, trainer Marguerite Weld, Dermot Weld, Bobby Dolan and Whacker O'Brien with Grey Swallow after winning the Budweiser Irish Derby at the Curragh in 2004.
Photograph Caroline Norris.

Trainer and breeder Marguerite Weld.

young Dermot followed proceedings, using the catalogue. He was sitting in the top row of seats, beside Mrs Healy from Waterford who was hard of hearing. The boy's shouted commentary to her provoked much amusement amongst the large attendance. Even now Dermot remembers that the filly sold for £200!

Whenever Dermot was at home from school he had to ride out and to help generally, and Marguerite would ride out too as it meant paying one less hand that day. Dermot's first race as an amateur jockey was in Ballinrobe – his mother did not see him ride as she was at home looking after the horses in the yard. However, she first saw him in the Amateur Bumper in Galway when he was 15. That day, he got his results in his Matriculation examination which gained him entrance to university. He was too young to begin his studies in veterinary science, and had to wait until he was 17. This meant he spent a year at home helping out and riding as an amateur.

The life of a trainer

There is a certain amount of rivalry amongst trainers, says Marguerite, as the competition for owners is very keen, with word of mouth and success being the main means of attracting business. The loyalty of the owners is very important to business. Marguerite recalls owners such as Major Douglas, who had a great horse called Maid of Galloway, Hugo Dolan, who had many successful horses, Michael Foley, whose horse Highfield Lad won the Galway Plate, and Buddy Flahavan of Kilmacthomas whose very good horse Decies was a Champion Two Year Old.

Jockeys play an important part in the success of a horse, and the Welds have had some very good jockeys over the years, Marguerite particularly recalls Martin Molony, T. P. Burns and Paddy Powell. They rode in her father's colours of blue with pink sleeves and a blue and gold quartered cap which are now Dermot's colours. The grooms and other people make up a good yard, people such as Billy Gainey, Ned Reilly, John Monahan, Tony O'Reilly, John Hughes, and many others.

Travelling with horses

Marguerite recalls that at one stage that there was no private transportation of horses. She remembers that there were three CIÉ horseboxes based in Kildare, and only these could be used. In addition, CIÉ would only collect horses within fifty miles of Dublin. Later private transport became available.

If a horse had been successful at home it might be taken outside the country. The first ever Irish horse to go the Washington DC International Stakes was Farney Fox, ridden by Tommy Burns and trained by the Welds in November 1963. The horse was put in a cargo plane at Shannon Airport and flown to Baltimore, and then transported to the race at Laurel Park in Maryland, near Washington, DC. The owner, Matt Donnelly, proprietor of the Anchor Hotel in Dublin, and trainer Charlie Weld also travelled. The winner was Bald Eagle, an American horse, and the Irish finished fourth. Dermot Weld recalls that this was at the time of the Bay of Pigs, when tensions between the USA and the Soviet Union were at their height. It was a tremendous diplomatic feat for the racecourse manager, John Di Shapiro, to get two Russian-owned horses to run in the race. Marguerite remembers that Michael O'Hehir provided the commentary on the radio, and that word about the Irish placing got around quickly in Kildare.

Farney Fox was an amazing horse, well-known in Ireland and England, and a favourite for any race. For a race at Birmingham the horse was sent over in a CIÉ horsebox. By the time the horsebox arrived it was too late to get into the Birmingham racecourse stables for the night, so the groom Joe Malone slept in the box with the horse. The next day, Farney Fox won the Triumph Herald Handicap with Tommy Burns on board. On another occasion, he came second in the Champion Hurdle at Cheltenham, ridden by Paddy Powell. Paddy did not like flying, so he travelled in the box. Thus, travelling in the horsebox were Farney Fox, Matt Donnelly the owner, Charlie Weld the trainer, Joe Malone the groom and Paddy Powell the jockey!

Breeding horses

Along with working at Rosewell as a trainer, Marguerite Weld also bred horses. She always had one or two mares with her father down the country. They owned the horses jointly, and after the death of her father, the horses were owned jointly with her brother, until he passed away. The yearlings would be sold. There was not much trade in foals at that time. After the death of her father and her brother, Marguerite bought Glenvale Stud near Carrick-on-Suir. This was later sold and it continues as a successful stud farm.

After Glenvale, Marguerite wanted a smaller place, but she decided to buy Piper's Hill in Naas, which was bigger than was required but which worked out very successfully. Later still came the move to Springbank, where she now has her stud.

In her first year there, she produced a horse called Grey Swallow which she bred and part-owned, and which became a champion two-year old. In the following year he won the Irish Derby, giving Marguerite her first classic winner as a breeder and part-owner. In 2005 Grey Swallow won the Group 1 Tattersall's Gold Cup under Pat Smullen, then he was raced in America where he won at Group 1 level, and he was subsequently sold as a stallion to Australia.

In 2006, Marguerite bred a filly called Nightime, one of the first crop of Galileo, who ran away with the Irish 1000 Guineas, winning by ten lengths. Nightime was trained by her son, Dermot, and it is hoped that the success will continue as Nightime will become a very fine mare for the stud.

Marguerite Weld is a leading breeder, and when Roll of Honour won the Grand Prix de Paris, this was one of her major successes. Tarry Flynn is also a very good Group horse that she owned and bred.

Recalling successful horses

From the early days, Marguerite remembers Lissenane as a very good horse. The mare Nightime, which won the 1,000 Guineas, was another, as was Enchanted Evening. Caumshinaun, named after a lake in the Comeragh mountains, and dam of Nightime, was another good horse recalled.

Choosing a name for a horse can be based on its breeding and also on placenames. Roll of Honour and Sylvia Fox, from the family of Farney Fox are names connected with breeding. Sometimes it is not possible to get the first choice of the name, and of the three names put forward none might be used. If a horse has died, the owner may be allowed to use the name again, but if it was a famous horse, the name would not be used until years later, Marguerite explains.

The secrets of a successful life

To what does Marguerite ascribe her success? She says to judgment and also a lot of luck with breeding. The most expensive suitable stallion could be picked, but then the horse might be infertile or there could be a problem with a foal. It is a very risky business with a lot of luck involved, but this can be offset with good care of the horses.

Until her retirement, Marguerite was still riding out at the Curragh, which she loved. When Dermot was young, and once she had help in the house to get him to school, she would ride out, and it certainly kept her fit. Having been brought up in a house where alcohol or cigarettes were never allowed, she never drank or smoked herself. There was a bottle of whiskey in the house but only for animals who were unwell. She certainly agrees that discipline played a major part in her life and success, and though everyone has difficulties in life, a life with horses means that others are coming on every year, so she has always looked forward, never back.

Marguerite has certainly packed a lot into a long and productive life. It may be said that, given the times, she was doing a man's job, but she points out that if you like working with horses and can handle people, it is a very good life. She feels that it is very important to hand-pick staff, as she has learned that there are some who cannot be taken on, and others who cannot be kept. Unfortunately, some people are capable of abusing a horse under cover, so one has to be alert at all times. It is a huge responsibility, but Marguerite always cared for the horses as though they had been her own. It really does not matter, she remarks, whether the owners are rich or poor, and indeed some of them were not too pleasant at times, but there is no doubt that the horses were all important.

As to results, which are crucial to a trainer's reputation, she explains that a horse would not be taken in unless she felt that she could do well with it. Winning a race and placing a horse is important, no matter the profile of the race.

In earlier years, Marguerite rode in point to point races, which she loved. She regarded these events as a 'bit of fun', whether she was riding for herself or for others. She would have loved to race on the flat around the track, but there were no 'lady riders' at that time.

Marguerite Weld has enjoyed a most successful and fulfilling life with horses, and she can look back on her life with great satisfaction and a quiet pride in her achievements. ■

Marguerite Weld, owner of Nightime, trained by her son Dermot, here with her grandchildren Kris (left) and Mark and jockey Pat Smullen, after winning the Irish 1,000 Guineas in 2006. *Photograph Healy Racing.*

Clem Magnier in 1979. *The Irish Field.*

CHAPTER 2

CLEM MAGNIER

You learn by your mistakes, and if you don't you're a bloody fool!

Clem Magnier was born near Fermoy in County Cork. His father, Michael J. Magnier ran several successful businesses in the town, including a hardware store, an undertaker's and a stud farm. Clem's mother was a member of the Kearney family from Kerry. The stud farm is now owned by John Magnier, who is the son of Clem's eldest brother Tom. Of necessity, Clem rode ponies from an early age – there were no cars on the road and the only means of transport were bicycles, pony and trap, horseback or shanks' mare!

Clem's education was not without incident, and he freely admits that he was not a scholar. He was expelled on his first day at Loreto Convent, Fermoy; apparently he kicked one of the religious sisters on the shins! He then attended the Christian Brothers' School in Fermoy; and later Ring College in Dungarvan. Clem believes that, at this time, plans may have been afoot to prepare him for the priesthood, and he was sent to Mount St Alphonsus, the Redemptorist school in Limerick. The plan did not succeed. He next attended Mount St Joseph's, the Cistercian school in Roscrea, which he loved, and he completed his secondary education at St Colman's College in Fermoy.

At seventeen, Clem began work on his father's stud farm of 180 acres and about six stallions. One of these was Cottage, which sired a number of great National Hunt horses which were subsequent

Grand National and Cheltenham winners, such as Cottage Rake and Lovely Cottage. Clem's father was very successful at buying young horses and training them as hunters or trap horses. He was contracted to collect the mail from the post office in Fermoy every night at 7 p.m., and deliver it to the station in Mallow in time for the midnight mail train to Dublin. This journey required two horses to pull the heavy car every night over steep hills and in all weathers.

Meanwhile, Clem was hunting twice a week with the Avondhu, Duhallow and United Hunts. He also went racing, and he sometimes took a day off to cycle to Killarney races. He considered the journey to Mallow races just a short ride, being only eighteen miles from home! He worked with his father for eleven years, and he explains that while their rapport was not strong generally, they had an excellent relationship where horses were concerned.

Unlike the situation in Britain, horse racing continued in Ireland during the years of the war, although Clem recalls that there were many restrictions due to shortages. Transport was particularly difficult, and for point to point races, the horse would be led to the race behind a pony and trap or a bicycle. Clem recalls his father taking a mare to a point to point at Ballynoe, which she won, and she was then required to pull the sidecar home. He also recalls running a horse for George Ainscough of Cork at Tramore races. He led the horse from Clonmel to Tramore, the race was run and the horse led home again. If a race was some distance away, the horse would be transported the night before and stabled overnight, with its feed brought on Clem's back on his bicycle. He would then cycle home to look after the other horses, returning the next day for the race. Both people and horses needed to be tough and fit in those days, he declares.

Going out on his own

In his late twenties, Clem decided to make his own way. His brother Tom ran the business in town, Paddy was a Redemptorist priest, and Michael was a doctor. He recalls that his father promised him that the farm would be his, but refused to put this in writing,. He then gave his father twelve months' notice and, when this expired, he left home on his bicycle, carrying with him only his suitcase and 30 shillings.. He set out for the races at Limerick Junction and then moved on to Dublin, travelling free whenever he was able. He bears no ill will towards his father, saying only that each had their own way.

He lived for three years at the Dolphin Hotel in Dublin, where bed and breakfast cost seven shillings and sixpence per night. He managed to eke out a living through betting and card playing, essentially living on his wits during this time.

Beginning as a trainer

When he was thirty-one years of age, Clem was contacted by his brother Tom who had inherited the farm. Tom offered him a horse to train, to which Clem agreed. He went to live with his sister and her family near Kilsheelan, and thus began his training career.

His first horse, Cavaliero, owned by his brother Tom, won its race on the first three outings. Clem also ran him in the Galway Plate, and the horse was then sold to Dorothy Paget for £10,000, a considerable sum in those days. His brother gave Clem £1,000 from the sale, and this was the beginning of his success story. Clem remembers Tom as a very fair man, though not a gambler like himself. It was vital to place a horse correctly, he explains, as in those days the stake money was not large so betting was important in order to make money. He often lost money but would recover and try again; "You learn by your mistakes and if you don't, then you're a bloody fool", he says. Clem is not one to mince his words and he calls a spade a spade!

His second owner was a Major who was based not far from Kilsheelan. This horse also won and was subsequently sold on. His third horse was Overshadow, a grey that Clem had exchanged with a man in Northern Ireland, at a cost of about £100. The horse had at one time been owned by Timmy Hyde, a Grand National jockey. Clem recalls that the horse arrived in very poor condition and no-one was able to ride him. He concentrated on getting the horse into prime condition, spending time on this and, crucially, gaining the horse's trust. Its first win was a two-mile bumper at Leopardstown, with his brother-in-law, Des Flynn, on board. Later the horse was sold to John A. Wood of Cork. Overshadow won the Irish Grand National at Fairyhouse in 1953, ten days after coming fourth in the Aintree Grand National.

Clem was now training seven or eight horses and, with his sister and her family, he moved into a property situated between Clonmel and Kilsheelan. Here there was a paddock and a large shed, which he converted into stables. A farmer nearby allowed him to use a field for training the horses, in return for £10 a winner, and he was also fortunate in his sister and his friends, such as Frank Carroll, a dentist from Clonmel, Arthur Morris, and his brother-in-law Des Flynn, who rode out the horses – this helped to keep costs down.

Training horses

Every trainer has his preferred methods, and few people train or work horses in the same way, Clem explains. Using Overshadow as an example, he reflects that with some horses, a robust approach is most effective, while with others, kindness works best. Whether you are dealing with difficult people or difficult horses, you have to cope, and work with what you're given. Some people can judge a horse and others cannot; this is a gift, Clem believes. He loves to look at horses, observing their movement, shape and temperament; all of which all add up. Pedigree, however, is not everything, he says. The best bred horse in the world might not be worth a penny, while its siblings might be top class.

Clem describes his training method as being a lot of long and slow work. He made his own all-weather gallops by ploughing up the ground and mixing in manure so that the ground would not dry out. The horses would then be run four miles at a hack canter, never trotting, a training method which would not be approved of by top trainers, he remarks. If a horse was not good enough, he would ask the owner to take it away, maintaining that "an empty house is better than a bad tenant".

His own place

Clem went on to buy a farm in Clerihan, County Tipperary, and he married Ursula Quirk from Carrick-on-Suir. He lived in the Ormond Hotel, Clonmel, while a house and stables were being built on the property. This was his first permanent stables, and three of his children were born here; the fourth was born in Rathvale, County Meath. His owners at this time included his brother Tom, Cork cattle-dealer Dan Horgan, John A. Wood, also in Cork, and Tom Good of Bandon.

While staying at the Ormond Hotel, Clem met with businessman J. C. Brady, and his manager who was a Frenchman. This man said that Teapot II could be bought for £700 and delivered to Ireland. The horse had already won a small flat race in the south of France. Clem says that this was the only horse he had ever bought sight unseen. When it arrived, he did some work with it and then left it rest for a year, after which it became the best hurdle horse in Europe, trained by Vincent O'Brien. The horse later sold for £10,000.

" I know what you want to do", said Tom [his brother]. "You want to train horses. **""**

Clem's reputation as a trainer was now growing, and the top jockeys began to come looking for rides. Over the years, the jockeys he employed included Doug Page, Lester Piggott, American Willie Shoemaker and Tommy Murphy who had worked for Fred Rimell in England. Clem also mentions Milo Walsh who was, he says, a "nice quiet rider" who loved horses.

As a successful trainer, Clem began to find that Tipperary was too far away from the big race meetings, and he deduced that it would be more convenient if he were to have stables in Meath. In about 1960 he began to search for a suitable property there.

Move to County Meath

The property in Clonmel was sold for £110,000, and this sum went towards the purchase price of Rathvale, the former racing stables of Reggie Walker, a top National Hunt trainer. However, the house, yard and gallops were in poor condition, and in need of renovation. During the 1980s, Clem also purchased nearby Trimblestown, bringing his property holdings to about 500 acres in all.

He could now increase the number of horses in training, though he says that this was a mistake. He was training 70 to 80 horses rather than 30 or 40, and he felt that owners were exploiting his expertise in preparing horses for winning, and then, just before they became successful, removing them, thinking they could do the winning themselves! As an example of this, he recalls an owner from Northern Ireland, for whom he got the horse ready, working on him and reducing his handicap. The owner then arrived with a horsebox and took the horse away – but he was never to win again. Clem recalls that, in fact, only one horse won a race after being removed from his stables.

Clem and his wife Ursula.

Michael, Clem and John Magnier.

Trainer Clem Magnier

Colin (left), Clem, Julie, Susie, Ursula and Avril.

The young Magniers: Bessy (left), Tom, Mary,
Michael (front row left), Nora, Granny, Clem and Paddy.

Losing his licence

Clem reflects on the great changes which have occurred in horse racing during his lifetime. He recalls that a certain snobbery prevailed in earlier days, and stewards could be prejudiced against certain individuals. He maintains that he was once unjustly warned off for three months, arising from an incident when he ran Dornoch at a Kerry course in a 1½ mile maiden hurdle, with the horse finishing down the field. Six weeks later, the horse ran in a two-mile race in Clonmel and won. Clem recalls that Judge Wylie was a senior figure in the Turf Club at the time and his son, John, was the handicapper. When Clem was warned off, he said to the stewards "Gentlemen, if I can't prove that the evidence against me is false I'll give you back my licence". He remembers Victor McCalmont saying that this was fair, but Judge Wylie asked Clem to leave. On the advice of his family, he did not take legal action as he had been warned off for only three months.

Having lost his licence, the horses had to leave his yard. They were put into a field owned by his brother, with Clem giving instructions from the road! From this group, Albergo won the 1959 Supreme Novices' Hurdle at Cheltenham with Doug Page on board.

Retirement

Clem Magnier retired about 25 years ago, relinquishing the reins to his son Colin. Colin Magnier was a very good amateur rider, winning the 1982 Champion Hurdle in Cheltenham on For Auction, for trainer Michael Cunningham. Clem now lives in Sarasota, Florida, and his passion now is for playing golf. Racing is different in America, he says, and he tends not to go. He has some advice for anyone thinking of getting into training racehorses. Looking after horses is hard work, he counsels, they need constant checking and one must always be observant to discern whether or not they are happy. It is also important to remember that the business is something of a lottery. He has seen many changes in the industry, not all for the better. For example, the stewards recently raised the weight for flat horses, but lowered it for National Hunt races. He disagrees with this decision, believing that it exposes a lack of knowledge and experience.

Clem Magnier does not claim to be ambitious, though naturally he loved to win; if he came second or third he always made a point of congratulating the winner, he says. His love of horses has been a constant in his long and productive life. ■

The Magnier clan: Michael (left), Bessy, Tom, Paddy, Nora, Clem and in the front is Mary, Michael J. and Birdie (Elizabeth) on Tom Magnier's wedding day.

Teapot, Overshadow and Prince of Devon, with Jimmy Long and the Maher brothers.

Luke Mullins in 1988.

CHAPTER 3

LUKE MULLINS

❝ The Galway shop proprietor
told me that the races week was better than any
other month of the year. **❞**

PROFILE

Luke Mullins

**Newbridge
Co. Kildare**

Born:
1922

Occupation:
**Racecourse
manager**

Luke Mullins was brought up in Doninga, County Kilkenny, on a farm bordered by County Carlow and the River Barrow. In his life he has been involved in agriculture, been a member of the Defence Forces and worked in and enjoyed racing and all that the sport of kings has to offer.

The middle child in a family of seven, his father owned a sizeable farm, on which he grew malting barley and oats for feed both before and after the economic war of the 1930s. Luke recalls that his father's farm was one of the test sites for growing sugar beet. In these earliest days of sugar manufacturing in Carlow, the beet was loaded for transport by canal barge from an old quay on the farm. He also remembers the excitement of seeing an aeroplane land on the farm's thirty-acre field on two occasions. This field was also used for point to point racing, as the hunt was allowed to go over the farm land. Luke remarks that the point to point originated as "a bit of fun and entertainment" – a reward for those property owners who permitted the hunt to ride over their lands. The horses, which were mainly hunters, took part in point to points in those days, and had to have a hunter certificate signed by the Master of the Hunt.

Luke studied agriculture at the old Albert College in Glasnevin in Dublin, which was part of UCD at that time. He remembers, shortly after the outbreak of the Second World War, hearing the German bombers attack the North Strand and not really knowing what was happening. He watched the searchlights rake the sky, and heard the anti-aircraft guns and the eerie whistling of the bombs as they fell.

The Army

During the Emergency in 1941, Luke decided to join the Irish Army. It was a time, he recalls, when many young men were joining up, either with the Irish or British armed forces. Luke was commissioned as a temporary officer and spent much of his army life at the Curragh Camp. He was sometimes rostered to supervise the two internment camps: Number 1, also known as "Tintown", was where Irish citizens who were known republicans were interned, and Number 2, nicknamed "K-Lines", contained Allied and German internees.

During the war years, Luke hunted mainly with the Naas Harriers. Those were extraordinary times. There were very few cars on the roads and petrol was rationed. Only doctors, vets and some other professions could get a petrol allowance but this did not deter the horse-racing fraternity. People from Kilkenny and further afield would cycle to Punchestown for meetings. He recalls watching Marguerite Weld winning the Ladies' Race in the point to point at Punchestown for a number of years in succession. Another competitor of note was Mrs Marshall, the mother of Brian Marshall, a well-known jump jockey in England, who rode side-saddle in show jumping.

When the war ended, Luke remained in the army as a commissioned officer. He was the only officer at the Curragh Camp who stabled his horse there, until Colonel Jack Lewis came to the Curragh from the Equitation School and also did so. In earlier times, most officers would stable their own horses at the Curragh Camp. At one time, an officer could automatically obtain an amateur rider's licence, and was permitted to train his horse on the gallops controlled by the Turf Club on the Curragh plain.

Luke resigned his commission in 1970. With his wife, Rita, one of the Ryans from Newbridge, and their four children, they moved to Galway to begin a new chapter with Luke taking up the role as manager of the Galway races. The Ryan family in Newbridge were business people and farmers, and Luke's father-in-law had some horses in training on the Curragh.

The Galway races

His appointment at Galway racecourse meant learning new skills in a world outside the Army, and he remarks, "You never stop learning". He reflects on the discipline which is such a major part of a soldier's life and which encourages a methodical approach to work, and an ability to manage people. This stood him in good stead in his new role.

A number of permanent staff were employed to maintain the racecourse at Galway, and were effective and did much good work; they were local people, many of them small farmers. Although Ballybrit was less than three miles from Galway city centre, it was then as rural as Connemara. Luke remembers a laneway leading out from Galway to the racecourse, crossing a farm where the Digital factory later stood, and passing 'Mary Burke's stile'. It is not that long ago, he says, since the horses would be stabled in Galway city, as there were no stables on the racecourse, and walked along this laneway to the races.

For its time, he says, Galway racecourse was in good condition, though the old grandstand was in a precarious state. For the Irish racing fraternity at that time, shelter was not a priority, although most tracks had covered stands though some were open, and in fact, still are.

The major attraction of the Galway races, both then and now, was its history, reputation and tradition; a feature not associated with all racecourses. Luke recalls a bank manager in Galway telling him that he met many of his clients only once a year, during race week!

The late Lord Killanin was chairman of the racecourse committee. The committee was proactive, and Luke was fortunate to be given freedom and encouragement to make improvements to the racetrack and facilities for the public. He remembers Lord Killanin as a very intelligent man who understood people and knew how to handle meetings. The committee had begun to hold a September race meeting the year before Luke arrived. Heretofore, there had been the three days of Galway race week and once that was over, the racecourse was closed down for the remainder of the year. A development plan was initiated to increase racing days and improve facilities. As part of the improvement plan, the old stand was demolished and rebuilt and a new weigh room and office accommodation were added. However, this improvement was not to "Ascot standards", Luke points out, because the money simply was not available.

In order to secure funding for the restoration, Luke and the racecourse accountant had many meetings with the late Pat Walsh, secretary of the Racing Board, in relation to grant funding. They succeeded in securing a sixty percent grant on any "improved work", with the racecourse committee providing the remaining forty percent. They then went looking for about £90,000, and the first port of call was the bank manager. Money was promised but with very onerous conditions, which were considered unreasonable. When another bank was supportive, the original bank quickly reconsidered, with less harsh conditions.

In the early 1970s there were two major races at Galway racecourse: the Galway Plate and the Galway Hurdle. Then the success of the Galway races depended on the Plate, which was the older race for which Galway is famed in song and story. The Hurdle had its origins in the early 1900s. Growth of the festival involved extending the number of racing days at Galway to provide new attractions for punters. Luke remarks that naming a race meeting a 'festival' does not make it one, but it is true for the Galway races, which he feels has a definite similarity with Listowel. The importance to the economy should not be forgotten. Luke recalls that the summer festival meeting was good for the city. He remembers buying a newspaper in a local shop just before the summer festival in the 1970s. The proprietor remarked that he was getting in his orders for merchandise at that stage, and that the races were "a better week than any other month of the year".

Betting

A good pitch at the Galway races was quite valuable to a bookmaker. Luke tells the story of a bookmaker from Tuam who changed his pitch at Galway to a much better site, and was gratified with the increase in bets he was taking; the money was coming in as fast as he could take it.

On the question of gambling on the racecourse in earlier days, he says that it is difficult to compare it with the present time as the entire process has changed. Before internet and telephone gambling, bets went solely to a bookmaker or the Tote on the racecourse. In addition, it is hard to estimate whether betting was heavier in the 1970s and 1980s than it is now, as additional racing days have been added since then, which had an effect on the amount of money in circulation.

Generating income

Luke is in no doubt that advertising played a part in the increasing success of Galway races. He sought advice on the most effective type of advertising, and was advised that television exposure was very important. In Ireland at that time, only one television and one radio channel existed, which made the advertising process and the placing of the budget very simple. Also,

> " He remembered the faction fights, and the strong men who would have their coats thrown on the ground. If you wanted to take him on you put your foot on the coat. "

it was known that a large proportion of the punters came from Northern Ireland, so they advertised on Downtown Radio in Belfast. He feels that the whole advertising aspect would be much more challenging nowadays. Player Wills sponsored a race at the July-August meeting and had a competition each year. Luke says the entries were analysed by address, and it was found that not alone did visitors come from all parts of Ireland but from Great Britain and the USA.

The Galway tent

As the Galway festival developed, Luke felt there would be good demand for corporate entertainment and sponsorship. Digital became sponsors of the Galway Plate, using the race to market their products. The marketing department at Digital made it clear that it was important for them to work in an informal atmosphere, getting their most important clients out of their offices and into a hospitality environment. The marketing arm of Digital used such a facility at the races. A senior executive from Waterford Crystal told Luke that the same process was followed at Cheltenham. There were no permanent buildings suitable for this purpose and tentage filled the gap.

The tent was sizeable, and a number of other companies took tables to host their guests. Luke acknowledges that the Galway races were an annual meeting place for many, and this developed further as companies and political parties were linked with the event.

Charlotte Street, Newbridge, County Kildare, showing Ryans of Newbridge in 1960s (on right).

Luke Mullins with his wife Rita.

Luke Mullins.

Other activities at Galway

Many other events took place during race week at Galway. Luke recalls that, as a newcomer to Galway, his initial reaction to the infield was that it was unsightly and full of litter, and he thought that perhaps it should be discontinued. Not long after this, he attended Phoenix Park races and saw no litter there. However, over time, he came to understand that the infield was important as a place where young people were introduced to the concept of the Galway races; it was a key part of the meeting with its carnival atmosphere and long tradition. Once, while walking down the enclosure, Brigadier Edmond Mahony told Luke that as a teenager at the Galway races, he watched the "trick-of-the-loop" and the "three-card-trick" men in the infield, and he claimed that Luke, as a native of the Pale, would probably not understand this! Another Galway gentleman recounted tales of the faction fights at the racecourse in times past, and the strongmen who could be taken on with a challenge.

Tradition and duty

The committee members at Galway were passionate about the racecourse, and Luke recalls their tremendous loyalty and involvement. He remembers that a member once approached him requesting that Luke inform the chairman of his wish to resign. This gentleman had been a member for twenty years, coming from a background where it is assumed that it is one's duty to serve if one has something to offer. When he spoke to Luke, he felt that he had fulfilled this requirement and could now retire. Such was the sense of duty which prevailed at that time.

Luke's wife Rita also played her part in the success of the races. Every race day, she made a point of informally meeting as many race goers as possible. Luke says that he himself always ensured he acknowledged every person he passed, and he emphasises that service and attention to the customer is essential. On race days, the chairman would assign specific duties to members of the committee; some would oversee turnstiles and entry to the course, while others would be deployed around the enclosure at specific points. Luke believes that people recognised and appreciated the attention to the customer that this arrangement implied.

Retirement

Luke retired in early 1989 and now looks back on his years at Galway as a wonderful period, when there was an excitement to life; racing attendance and betting records were regularly broken. The Galway races, he says, truly hold a most important place in the Irish social calendar, and in the hearts of race-going people everywhere.

As he reflects on the glory days, he has no regrets about his tenure in Galway and he attributes his success to his army background, his love of racing and the teamwork of everyone involved. Horse racing is a great sport he says, though recent trends such as fashion competitions and aggressive advertising are disappointing – he regrets the fact that racing can no longer seem to stand on its own. ∎

At the rail: P. J. Prendergast, Bridie Healy (Pallastown Castle), Rita Mullins, cousin Mary Coleman, at the Thyestes Chase, Gowran Park.

An Coláiste Mileata, 6th Staff Course, 1961-62. Captain L. A. Mullins (back row, 2nd from left).

Vincent and Jacqueline O'Brien.

CHAPTER 4

JACQUELINE O'BRIEN

" It must have been a surprise to everyone that this very eligible Irish horseman was whipped off by an Australian who knew nothing about his profession. **"**

J acqueline Wittenoom grew up in Western Australia, where her paternal ancestors had emigrated from London in 1829. Her great-great-grandfather, John Burdett Wittenoom, a widower and the first colonial chaplain in Perth, brought his four sons to Western Australia because he felt they would have a better chance of acquiring land there. His ancestors had come from Holland to London in about 1668.

The 1820s was a difficult time after the Napoleonic Wars and the economic situation in Europe was very poor. The Rev. Wittenoom received 5,000 acres of land in Western Australia in recompense for all that he had brought with him on the journey from England. He settled in Perth, and built the first church on the site where the Anglican cathedral now stands. Only recently, Jacqueline's agreement has been sought in order that his remains may be disinterred and placed in a purpose-built sepulchre in the cathedral.

Jacqueline has undertaken research on the history of her family. The Rev. Wittenoom's grandsons, Edward and Frank, owned two million acres of the dry sheep-producing land before they reached the age of 21. Her grandfather, Edward, and father, Charles, were both members of Parliament (the Western Australia Legislative Council) at the same time; her grandfather was President of the Legislative Council. They were also involved in other areas such as farming and gold mining. Jacqueline knew and recalls her grandfather Edward quite well until his death in 1936. Both he and her grand-uncle, Frank, were men of authority in Western Australia.

Jacqueline's father, Charles Horne Wittenoom, was a Member of the Western Australian Legislative Council, and her mother, Patricia Hanrahan, had been a schoolteacher. For part of the year, the family lived in Albany, on the south coast but they also spent time at Muralgarra, in the Geraldton area, a sheep station of about ¼ million acres. The front gate was about twenty miles from the front gate to the front door, in a region which was very dry and hot. Fortunately, Jacqueline's mother was interested in education, for which she has always been grateful. She and her brother were called "children of the bush" and their school lessons would come in an envelope which was dropped at the small railway station every fortnight. She later attended the Loreto Convent boarding school in Perth, which was run by Irish nuns from Rathfarnham. Then Jacqueline studied Economics at the University of Western Australia, and was awarded a scholarship to study employment and trade. She spent a year sitting in arbitration courts as part of her studies, and then began her career as an economist.

In 1951, Jacqueline and her mother made a trip to Europe, during which they visited relatives in Northern Ireland. One evening, Jacqueline was dining in the Russell Hotel in Dublin with a friend named Waring Willis, an amateur rider. At another table Vincent O'Brien was dining alone. Willis was often used by Vincent as a jockey and Waring invited him to join them at their table. As Jacqueline recalls, Vincent was initially reluctant, as he had to be up early for the races the following day, but he accepted the invitation. Eventually, just he and Jacqueline remained at the table, and he invited her to accompany him to the races the following day. Thus began a whirlwind courtship. Jacqueline was invited to visit Vincent's family home at Cashel in County Tipperary, where she met his two brothers and his mother, whom she recalls as being a very intelligent and charming woman. Jacqueline stayed at a nearby hotel, as construction work was being undertaken on the O'Brien home. Her mother had already returned home to Australia, and so Jacqueline also travelled back to tell her parents the news of her impending marriage. On her return to Ireland, she and Vincent were married in the University Church in Dublin, and the wedding reception was held in the Shelbourne Hotel.

Over the following years, Jacqueline's parents often visited Ireland. She smiles as she recalls that her father could never understand how in Western Australia one sheep needed twenty acres, and in Ireland there were ten sheep per acre!

The O'Briens in Cork

Vincent O'Brien's family came from Clashganiff near Buttevant, a part of Cork that was well known for horse breeding and racing. She recalls that Vincent would talk about his childhood, and the stories of how the children, returning from school, would jump over the ditches to avoid the Black and Tans going past in their trucks. During the Economic War of the 1930s the cattle could not be exported and were not worth the price of their skins, and he would describe the desperate poverty of that time. Vincent began training horses immediately after the Second World War. On his first trip to England, he travelled to Cheltenham in 1948 with

Cottage Rake, owned by Frank Vickerman. Jacqueline recalls that Vincent was quietly confident that Cottage Rake had a winning chance. The horse was walked to the train, then taken onward to Cheltenham by boat and train, and both Vincent and Cottage Rake arrived in good order. This was the biggest steeplechase of the year, "and an Irishman had come more or less on foot with his horse!" Vincent was unfamiliar with the racecourse at Cheltenham, and he was not sure even where to stand to watch the race. Cottage Rake ran with Aubrey Brabazon as jockey, and they were first past the post to win the Gold Cup. Vincent brought the horse back on two further occasions, to win again in 1949 and 1950. Jacqueline maintains that this run of success gave the Irish a huge boost in confidence.

Ballydoyle

In 1951, Vincent O'Brien moved from Buttevant to Ballydoyle, County Tipperary, just before he had first met Jacqueline. What had been a farm in Ballydoyle had to be transformed into a training facility and Jacqueline arrived into the middle of this transformation. As she recalls, everything had to be done by hand, and the gallops were made by knocking down ditches between fields. She remembers that the house was not in a very good condition, but the horses were ensconced in new stables!

Jacqueline admits that she knew nothing about horses at that time, and that she still would not consider herself to be a judge of a horse. She recalls that on her first visit to Ballydoyle, she was in the sitting room with an Englishman. They were both waiting for Vincent. The gentleman had travelled from England to see Cottage Rake, so Jacqueline obliged him by taking him out to the stables where Vincent had shown her the horse the previous day. The man appeared quite surprised and somewhat bemused. Shortly afterwards he had to leave to catch a train; later Jacqueline discovered that he was one of the leading racing journalists in England, and that she had shown him the wrong horse! As she says with a laugh, she really knows very little about horses, even now.

At Ballydoyle, life was very busy after Vincent and Jacqueline's marriage. A lot of hard work had to be done to get the place in order, and four children arrived fairly quickly, and another later on. Jacqueline did much of the secretarial work, but she was not involved in the work in the yard, which Vincent and his brother Dermot ran. She remarks that the brothers complemented each other very well, as Dermot had commonsense and was quite placid, while "Vincent was the fiery one". Another brother Phonsie, an excellent amateur rider, was also involved. He had been riding for Vincent for years. Vincent encouraged his children to go out with him in the mornings, though they would sometimes become bored and go off to do more exciting things. The children did not have much exposure to cities, or to holidays away. The three girls all hunted and had show ponies, but the two boys, at that stage, were less keen.

Jacqueline always enjoyed going to the races if they had horses running. She knew about the horses they were training and was interested in how they ran; however, she had little interest in form or in betting. Her favourite horse was The Ministrel, which had four white legs, believed to be unlucky. The children had a nanny who was very superstitious which made things complicated for her on race days, she says. However, Vincent had no time for superstition, thinking it ridiculous.

A trainer has to work hard, and owners can be quite demanding, often expecting the trainer to socialise with their friends after racing. This was difficult as Ballydoyle was a long drive from Dublin and the horses had to be worked early the next morning. Horse racing has a social side, Jacqueline explains, especially at the higher grade of racing such as at Ascot or the Derby and presented difficulties as most trainers would prefer not to stay late for drinks and dinner with the owners, but to get home to look after the horses. However, getting owners is the hardest thing a trainer has to do. The social aspect was a very important part of Jacqueline's life, and it was easier for her as she did not have responsibility for the horses as well. In addition, she had experience of getting along with people as her father was a parliamentarian – as she says, it's the same kind of thing, getting votes or getting owners!

> **" I can only remember Vincent going into another trainer's yard once in Ireland - Mickey Rogers', and once in England - Cecil Boyd-Rochfort's. "**

Training is constant, unceasing work, and Vincent certainly never sat back. He was constantly investing in the business, making new gallops or putting up new buildings. Jacqueline remembers that he was never satisfied, but constantly aspired to better things. Looking back she says that unlike most trainers, he was never interested in what others did. As far as she recalls, the only trainer's yard in Ireland that he ever set foot in was that of Mickey Rogers, and in England, Sir Cecil Boyd-Rochfort's just once. Jacqueline remarks that he did not find it easy to talk to people and she was some use as a sounding board – where he could assess different plans for the horses.

Troubled times

Vincent lost his trainer's licence in 1960, an event which marked an appalling period in his and Jacqueline's lives. Following a race at the Curragh, a letter arrived which stated that Vincent's horse had been doped in a small race, and he was to appear before the stewards at an appointed time. He also received a message with the instruction that nothing was to be said about the matter. On the appointed day, Vincent met the stewards and learnt all the details.

The horse concerned had been in the Curragh yard the night before the race but there had been no night watchman on duty, and all the gates were open. Vincent and Jacqueline thought that perhaps someone had 'got' at the horse during the night. The certificate of dope stated that approximately 1/500th of a gram of a substance resembling methylamphetamine had been found. They decided to look further into the matter and discovered that according to the experts, including the expert at Glaxo, it was not a certificate of dope at all, as at the time, it was not possible to isolate 1/500th of a gram of any substance. Then a dossier of support built up,

Jacqueline O'Brien, photographer and author.

John and Mary McShain, owners of Ballymoss, with Jacqueline and Vincent O'Brien.

including letters from the New York Jockey Club and the French Jockey Club agreeing with the experts. In addition, it was not sufficient to find a substance *resembling* something; what has to be found is the substance itself.

Vincent had this dossier of documents, and opinions from forensic scientists, but the stewards would not take heed. Under the rules of racing back at that time, it was not permitted to take legal action against the stewards. However, it was discovered that Vincent had been accused under a rule which stated that he had personally doped the horse, and not under the rule that he was responsible as a trainer for the occurrence of the doping. During this time, Vincent and Jacqueline had to leave their home with their young family, and they remained away for six months until Joe McGrath said they could return, on condition that Vincent did not go into the yard.

Vincent then took the stewards to the Supreme Court as he had been accused under the wrong rule. Jacqueline acknowledges the great help they received from Judge Lavery, the public and also from one of the stewards. It was not until they were on the steps of the courthouse that the stewards backed down. Vincent received an apology and confirmation that he had done nothing wrong. Jacqueline is sure that if they had not proceeded with the court case as they did, Vincent would never have trained again. She relates that even before this terrible time, Vincent had lost his licence for three months on the grounds that three of his horses had run inconsistently, and as a result, he was not allowed to enter a racecourse anywhere. There was great jealousy in Ireland, Jacqueline maintains, because he was so successful, and successful in a way that could not be explained. Vincent had taken over to England a previously unsuccessful horse named Hatton's Grace, which won the Champion Hurdle at Cheltenham three years in succession from 1949 to 1951. Vincent won the Cheltenham Gold Cup for a fourth time with Knock Hard in 1953. Between 1953 and 1955, he won the Grand National at Aintree three times with Early Mist, Royal Tan and Quare Times. Jacqueline feels that it could not be admitted that he was a very good trainer, because if it was, others would look less good by comparison. Just after Vincent got his licence back Larkspur won the Derby.

Subsequently, the relationship between Vincent O'Brien and the Turf Club improved. The Turf Club had been the first European body to introduce dope testing, but it had not been set up properly, nor had it any safeguards to protect an innocent person. Members had been opinionated, and had not sought assistance. Vincent's case was responsible for making the rules better so some good came out of it. Living with that tension was very difficult, Jacqueline recalls, but then, training horses is also full of tension – a good horse can go lame, the condition of a track might not suit on the day, and any number of variables can influence an outcome.

There were other contentious occasions for the O'Briens, such as when Kings Lake, ridden by Pat Eddery, won the Irish 2,000 Guineas at the Curragh in 1981. The runner-up was To-Agori-Mou, which belonged to Captain Boyd-Rochfort. However, it was decided that Kings Lake had gone across the course, and the win was not allowed. Jacqueline remembers that Vincent went outside after the decision was made. He walked up and down the road behind the stands, and then came in to tell the stewards that he was going to object to their decision. By this stage, legal representation at stewards' inquiries was allowed. Having watched the film, Vincent was quite convinced that Kings Lake should keep the race as were the stewards when the case was heard again. Naturally, Captain Boyd-Rochfort was very angry when the decision was made in favour of Kings Lake. It was quite unusual for a decision to be overturned in a classic race.

Moving on

In the 1950s Vincent began training horses for flat racing. Ballydoyle had high-powered American owners, whom Jacqueline looked after while Vincent looked after their horses. She acknowledges that she developed a conversational veneer which covered her lack of knowledge of the equine world! The O'Briens bought yearlings to be trained in Ireland for American owners, many of these were wealthy and important. Much of the stock in America came from European mares and stallions, bought in the previous decades. At one time, an owner and friend named Jack Mulcahy enquired of Vincent about his income from training, and when Vincent replied that he got his percentage fee as did all the other trainers, Jack thought that this situation was ridiculous, because the value of a horse could increase from £1 million to £30 million, and the trainer would not benefit. From then onwards, Jacqueline explains, Jack Mulcahy gave Vincent an automatic share in all the horses he bought. Later, Vincent joined with John Magnier and Robert Sangster and, as a syndicate, they would buy yearlings themselves, race them, and then send them to stud, a practice continued by John Magnier since Vincent's death. However, she continues, the Arabs then arrived, and their money was unlimited – they were difficult to compete with. Vincent trained some horses for Sheikh Mohammed, who invited him and Jacqueline to Dubai on a number of holidays. Jacqueline remembers that the Sheikh thought Vincent was a good horseman, and Vincent was interested to see his camels. The Sheikh also took him shooting in the desert, and was very impressed with Vincent's ability to spot a bird which was the same colour as the rock.

Jacqueline remembers Vincent as being very observant of people, horses and nature. He could be particular about details, and was always very well dressed. His staff would call him "the Fuhrer" because he was strict and demanded a very high standard. Horses had to be impeccably turned out and everything had to be perfect. Jacqueline recalls that this was at a time when other people were not so careful; the horses were well-trained, but the standard of presentation was not considered so important. Similarly, racecourses had few facilities at that time in comparison to today. A bar, the stands and the roof were all that was available, but there was no great comfort at race meetings, Jacqueline recalls, which made entertaining foreign visitors more of a task.

Coolmore Stud

In 1971 Vincent bought Coolmore Stud, about seven miles from Ballydoyle. Jacqueline, while researching a book on her Australian great-grandfather, was fascinated to discover a family connection with the estate. A relative from Perth, William Burges, who had been one of the early pioneers in Western Australia, had become wealthy through sheep farming there, and had returned to Ireland and bought Coolmore. After he died it was sold and the money divided among his West Australian relatives.

At Coolmore, Vincent moved into breeding horses. Tim Vigors, who had been a Battle of Britain pilot during the Second World War, sold the property to Vincent, but he kept a small share in it. John Magnier was then brought in to manage the breeding farm. He later married Jacqueline and Vincent's daughter, Susan, and he and Robert Sangster subsequently became partners in the business. Coolmore became very successful. Jacqueline describes John as an extremely capable and astute individual. The three partners then decided to operate Coolmore in America and in Australia, and Coolmore is now the biggest bloodstock company worldwide.

In Jacqueline's opinion, the purchase by Vincent in Canada of Nijinsky was of real significance to the enterprise. The horse was a son from the second crop from Northern Dancer. Vincent had gone to the Windfield's stud in Canada for Charles Engelhard, the American industrialist, who had picked out a horse by Ribot that he wanted Vincent to buy. As things turned out, Vincent much preferred a Northern Dancer colt, later named Nijinsky, which he then trained in Ireland. Northern Dancer had not done particularly well in North America but, Jacqueline points out, out of 2,000 horses in one Goffs sales catalogue, about 1,200 went back to Northern Dancer. Nijinsky's success was initially responsible for the popularity of the Northern Dancer blood line and had a colossal effect on breeding in Europe; it also made Coolmore a success story. Sadlers Wells by Northern Dancer was the champion stallion of Europe for fifteen years. Today, almost every horse in Europe has Northern Dancer blood in its veins.

When Nijinsky won the Derby, Charles Engelhard had to be presented to and shake the hand of the Queen Mother. He was a large man, says Jacqueline, who walked with a stick. In the excitement of it all, his braces broke, and he had to hold up his trousers with his elbows while he shook the royal hand!

Queen Elizabeth II visited Coolmore in 2011, during her state visit to Ireland. This visit was a private event; she knew about the stud as she has had horses at Coolmore for a long time. John Magnier took her around the property at high speed in a golf cart. Then she had lunch with about twelve people, after which she left for Cork. Jacqueline remarks on the Queen's absolute passion for horses, and her tremendous admiration for anybody who is good with them.

Jacqueline has also met some other very interesting people, who have reached the pinnacle of their particular businesses. She remembers Mr Kline from Smith Kline & French, in particular, as one of the nicest men she has ever met. Other owners included Alice Du Pont Mills and John McShain, who built the Pentagon, the Lincoln Memorial and many other buildings in Washington, DC; he also renovated the White House. His horse Ballymoss was a great success on the flat. These important Americans approved of the O'Brien method of training, and they also liked the fact that racing in Ireland is on grass and that the horses were gently handled. In America, Jacqueline explains, racing on dirt is hard on the horses and winning quickly is more important than longer term plans.

Phoenix Park racecourse

Jacqueline recalls that Vincent would always be trying to improve the horse racing calendar, which he thought was poorly planned. He could see that the racing programme should have been compiled in a particular way, but it was difficult to get agreement. Vincent's favourite race was the National Stakes in September, which has now been called after him. It is the ideal race for two-year olds preparing them for the classic races in the following year.

In 1984, the Vincent O'Brien-trained Sadlers Wells, another progeny of Northern Dancer, won the inaugural running of the Phoenix Champion Stakes in September, the most valuable race ever run at that time in Ireland. This is a race that he decided was badly needed and is now one of the most important races in the flat racing programme. Though he invested hugely in the Phoenix Park racecourse by putting in new stands and so on, Vincent and the other investors lost heavily. Jacqueline feels that the situation was not attractive to the racing public – perhaps it was not on the right side of the river. The course was tight, and there was not a lot of room, but it was a lovely place, she says, quite quaint and old-fashioned. The Curragh was her own favourite racecourse; Vincent loved Ascot and on one occasion, he had seven winners from eight runners during the Royal festival.

Innovation

Jacqueline O'Brien reflects on the fact that her late husband always seemed to lead. He was the first to fly horses, the first to feed the horses three times a day, the first to breed from the Northern Dancer line and bring success to it. He was very particular about gallops. He experimented all the time trying to find a better surface to keep horses sound and in work whatever the weather.

He never wanted to train his horses on gallops which other people had provided, and over which he had no control, and for that reason, he did not choose to train at the Curragh. If a horse was highly strung, he would work it gently and perhaps on its own. He never wished to be part of a crowd, which is probably why a certain suspicion may have existed because the opposition in the racing world thought he was hiding away.

He was the first to fly horses, taking three runners by air to Cheltenham, which was thought extraordinary at the time. Jacqueline recalls his belief that to a horse, flying is the same as travelling in a horsebox. The aeroplane used was a converted bomber, and the horses entered through the nose of the plane. Later Vincent bought a plane called a Skyvan, a small plane so that it could land on the runway at Ballydoyle, and two horses at a time could get to the airport in England nearest the racecourse where they were to run. Obviously, this did not work with a large number of horses, though it was useful for a time as Vincent felt that it was very important to get a horse to a race in as fresh a condition as possible.

He was highly innovative in his ideas and methods, for instance, having music played to the horses in the stables to familiarise the horses with different sounds, so that the noises at race meetings would not disturb or surprise them. He was one of the first to weigh horses every week. With regard to exercising the horses, he never extended them fully at home, so there was always a bit in reserve. Jacqueline recalls that there were four easy fences going up a hill on the gallops. These were never very high, even if the horse was going to run in the Grand National. Vincent believed that if a horse was well and happy, he would jump higher on the day because of the crowds and the excitement of the occasion. However, if "the race" has already been run at home, the actual race itself would probably be a disappointment..

The jockeys who rode for Vincent included Lester Piggott, Pat Eddery, Liam Ward, T. P. Burns and John Reid. He had a very good relationship with Lester Piggott, Jacqueline remembers. She says that they would regularly be seen talking together on the racecourse, and people would wonder what they were discussing. She says that they would rarely speak about instructions for the race, but only about what races were coming up, and such matters. Vincent would have given his instructions on the telephone or in the weigh room beforehand. However he would feel a top jockey must be free to make his own decisions, depending on how a race is proceeding. Vincent always liked the Australian jockeys, says Jacqueline, because they were so well-trained, and were great judges of speed. She recalls some proud names such as Pat Glennon, 'Scobie' Breasley, Garnie Bougoure, and Jack Purtell.

Jacqueline O'Brien and her late husband Vincent have led remarkable lives, marked by hard work, endurance and accomplishment. The hugely successful Ballydoyle where Aidan O'Brien continues training with great success for John Magnier and his partners stands as a testament today to their joint endeavours: the gallops are as Vincent laid them out all those years ago when they were made with manpower and shovels. Coolmore Stud and Lyonstown also show today Vincent's immense foresight and skill in breeding horses as well as training.

When he retired Vincent said, 'Racing has been good to me enabling me to combine work with pleasure.' He always gave great praise to his brothers and his dedicated staff. He also always said that it gave him enormous satisfaction to have seen Irish racing and breeding become world-class industries. ∎

Jacqueline O'Brien holds future trainer David, while Vincent O'Brien looks on at Royal Tan with Liz and Sue on board.

Stan Cosgrove examining a horse at Moyglare Stud Farm.

CHAPTER 5

STAN COSGROVE

> " As long as Ireland is here and people are here, there'll be horse racing. "

PROFILE

Stan Cosgrove

Kildare

Born:
1927

Occupation:
Veterinary Surgeon

S tan Cosgrove trained as a veterinary surgeon just after the Second World War, and he has witnessed many changes and innovations in the treatment of thoroughbred horses during his long career.

His paternal grandparents had a typically Irish business, which combined a public house, grocery, drapery shop and dairy in Kildare town. His father Jimmy, a medical practitioner, was one of three sons, his two brothers became a veterinary surgeon and a pharmaceutical chemist. Stan's grandfather died in the 1890s, so his uncle Joe came home from Rockwell College to work in the drapery section of the business. However, it did not suit him as his interest was horses. When his mother sent him to buy a cow, he came home with a horse! Eventually, Joe became a vet. Jimmy, Stan's father, initially worked as a chemist in McHugh's in Kildare, and he went on to study medicine. Following his qualification, Jimmy worked as a GP in Newbridge, County Kildare.

Stan Cosgrove is one of six siblings. His brother Paddy was a doctor in Mansfield in the UK, and another brother Joe went into the pharmacy in Newbridge.

Stan married Maureen Keenan from Naas, whom he describes as the "greatest woman that ever lived – the best". Her father had owned drapery shops in County Kildare. Together Stan and Maureen reared a family of ten children. None of them have followed Stan into the veterinary business, and he thinks, perhaps this is because they have seen the long hours and hard work the job demands. Stan says that his late wife was a great support to him, although she did not get involved with his work. They lived in Kildare town in earlier days, though later he bought ten acres outside the town and built Troytown Veterinary Hospital, he then moved in the 1990s, to Barrow House in Monasterevin. Now he has a little apartment in Moyglare Stud Farm where he lives during the week, and at weekends his children take it in turns to spend time with him at his own house.

The business of being a veterinarian

Stan Cosgrove himself made the decision to become a vet, and, as he recalls, it was easier in those days to train to be a vet as there was no such thing as points for entry to college. He began his studies in 1946 in the veterinary college in Dublin, which was under the joint auspices of University College Dublin and Trinity College Dublin. He recalls being lectured in Anatomy by Professor Brown, in Physiology by Professor Nicholson, in Pharmacology by Frank Connolly, in Animal Management by Des O'Connor, in Pathology by Professor Kearney and Surgery by Professor McGeady, among others. He qualified as a veterinary surgeon in 1952.

After qualification, he worked as a locum for a brief period for Brendan Clarke in Athboy. This was to be his only experience of working outside of his own practice. His cousin, Fran, who was also a vet and the son of his uncle Joe, had died in 1947 from a kick to the head by a horse. The practice was then owned by another cousin, Maxie, along with Walt Davison. They employed an assistant, Bob McCaughey from Northern Ireland, to keep the practice going. Bob, whom Stan recalls as a very good vet, left the practice in 1952. Stan then began work in the practice, after his brief period of work experience in Athboy. He was now working for his cousin and Walt Davison who were based in Dublin, but effectively he was on his own in Kildare. He was thrown in at the deep end, and he wryly remarks that you learn very quickly by your mistakes.

Stan was working in general practice, mainly with large animals such as cattle, horses, sheep and pigs. In those days, he was on duty twenty-four hours a day, seven days a week. Stan recalls that in 1956 he got a radio telephone before even the ambulance service or the Garda Síochána. He was one of three vets in Ireland with this equipment – the others were William Baker in Bansha and a vet named Ryan in Fermoy. He says that the radio telephone, with its huge transmitter, was a great help to him in his work.

His cousin Maxie and Walter Davison parted company, and in 1956 Stan and Maxie along with Brendan Farrelly, Seán Collins, and Jim Kavanagh, formed another partnership called Riversdale Clinic. Stan was in Kildare while the other partners were in Dublin. At this stage he was covering Kildare and also going into Limerick. This arrangement continued until 1962 when Stan bought out the other partners. Stan was now his own boss.

He built an operating theatre and two recovery boxes behind his house in Kildare town. Horses suffer from colic when the gut becomes twisted and Stan began to do abdominal surgery, which was innovative at the time. There were no books available on the subject, and there were lots of failures with this new approach, but also some successes. At that time, he would go over to Mansfield to stay with his brother Paddy, and he discovered that there was a very good surgeon in the local hospital named Niall McQuaid. Stan would go into the theatre with Niall to learn from that environment about such things as asepsis and the 'human' approach to surgery.

In about 1970 Stan attended a course in orthopaedics in Davos in Switzerland. The Swiss, he explains, have huge expertise in orthopaedics as broken bones happen so frequently on the ski slopes. The old way of repairing a broken bone was with the use of a cast, which left a callus, and was not a neat repair. The Swiss developed an internal fixation system where the bone was compressed and thus the join would not be obvious later. People attended from around the world, both surgeons and vets. Stan was the first Irish resident surgeon, human or veterinary, to attend. This was confirmed by the famous Irish orthopaedic surgeon, Jim Sheehan, who came the following year. Later Stan returned to Davos to attend more advanced courses, as he was keen to add to his knowledge, and to become a better vet.

Thoroughbred horses, compared to other breeds, are very prone to shock, he explains, and while it is possible to quite successfully repair injuries below the hock and the knee, it is very difficult above the knee. After an operation, the danger point is in recovery when the horse tries to get up when coming around after anaesthesia. He recalls the New Bolton Centre in Philadelphia which developed a suit for the horse, that would then be floated in a pool so that it would not damage itself as it awoke from surgery.

Anyone dealing with a horse has to be careful, but if you let yourself think about the value of the animal, you would be driven crazy, he says. Stan's method was to treat all horses the same, and to do his best in their treatment. He acknowledges that sometimes a horse would have to be put down, and nowadays an injection is used. It can be upsetting to have to do this, he says, but depending on the injury it can be the most humane course.

Changes in veterinary practice

Today, Stan continues to offer some advice as a vet, though the Moyglare Stud now has a very good young vet named Katie Murphy. She does the routine work, and another vet named Ted Collins looks after the mares and does the vaccinations and so on.

Veterinary practice has changed a lot over the years, says Stan, and has advanced in certain ways. He acknowledges that there have been great advances in the treatment of colic. However, in some other areas there is little change, such as tendon damage from which a horse still needs a good year's rest in order to recover. With viruses and respiratory disease there has not been much progress. Nowadays, a lot more testing is done, and analytic equipment such as x-rays, artheroscopes, and fibroscopes have greatly helped with diagnosis. In earlier days, a joint had to be opened up, which was more invasive. Stan agrees that there has been good progress in the area of diagnostics, but he is not so sure that newly-qualified vets have the practical skills. He explains that in the early days, the development of diagnostic equipment came from human medicine, but medics can rely on a person giving information about a problem, while a horse cannot oblige!

Drugs in the sport

When asked whether there is a problem with the use or abuse of drugs in horse racing, he explains that no drugs can be used in Ireland and Europe, though it is a big problem in America. A lot of good horses were going to America in 1970s and 1980s, but this has stopped because of the economic downturn, and so they are staying in Ireland or going to places such as Japan. Examples of drugs used in America are Lasix, used for bleeders, and Bute for horses that are a bit stiff, but Stan emphasizes that their use would not be allowed here. The regime in Ireland is very strict, and if a horse is given something, even inadvertently, then the trainer is in trouble and at risk of losing his licence. The testing is very detailed, so it is important never to give in to temptation.

Moyglare Stud Farm

Walter Haefner, a Swiss industrialist, bought Moyglare Stud Farm in 1962, and Stan attended to the horses there. In 1971, he was asked to manage the farm, and he got on very well with Mr Haefner, who died in 2012 aged 101. His daughter Eva now owns Moyglare Stud Farm and is learning the business rapidly and is very easy to work with being understanding and generous. In 1972, Mr Haefner bought the most expensive brood mare in the world at a sale in Lexington, Kentucky, for $450,000. She was called What a Treat. He wanted the best and he could afford it, says Stan, as he was very wealthy. The mare turned out to be very successful, and she was the dam of the similarly very successful Be My Guest.

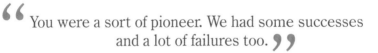

" You were a sort of pioneer. We had some successes and a lot of failures too. "

The breeding is researched by breeding expert Fiona Craig but Eva Haefner is now taking an active part as Stan has always done down through the years. He explains that with breeding, account has to be taken of the temperament of the mares, and there are also many other factors. Some of the most perfect horses are worthless, but then there could be not so good-looking horses that are fantastic. He does acknowledge the fact that there are people who have picked out more winners than others, but he points out the riskiness of the business when he says that only about five percent of horses win Group races. It is indeed a risky business, and there is no guarantee that money spent will give any return. This explains why owners have to be wealthy – there are no guarantees.

The management of Moyglare is straightforward. There are four teams. The stud team with Pat Farrell as the stud groom with a couple of people assisting him. The racing team breaks in all the yearlings, which are then ready to go to a trainer; this team is headed up by a great horseman,

Mad Hatters Race at the Phoenix Park in 1972, won by Joe McGovern.
Back row: Mick O'Toole (1st on left), John Mulhern (3rd from left); front row: Stan Cosgrove (extreme right)

Stan Cosgrove with Go and Go.

Student Stan Cosgrove at Veterinary College, Dublin,
being presented with a Gold Medal in 1945.

Stan Cosgrove at work in the 1960s.

Jimmy Feane and his group. Then there is the farm team made up of Frank Broad, Jack Walsh and Brendan Judge, and lastly the garden team of Patrick Codd and Eoin McEntee. In the office there are two excellent secretaries: Ita Murphy, who looks after all the financial matters and runs a tight ship, and Margaret Lundy, who looks after all the horse side of the business. They all run their own teams and Stan orchestrates. Stan maintains that they tell him what to do rather than the other way around. However, if something goes wrong, then the responsibility falls on him.

Others are also employed at the stud farm, such as the farrier Niall Foley from Dunshaughlin. His father worked there before him. Horseshoes have not changed too much over the years, although there are different kinds of shoe to help a horse. There are stick-on shoes now so that nails are not needed.

Since Stan began work at Moyglare, the acreage has almost doubled to the present 470 acres. Some of that land had to be bought up as fences or boundaries were not being properly kept. It is important to protect the horses from other animals, such as cattle, he says.

At the stud there are brood mares, foals and yearlings. The numbers are kept to about one hundred in all, which is a relatively small number compared to some other operations. There are some mares also at Ashford Stud in Lexington, and the foals are reared at the farm. On January 1st they become yearlings, and in about October, the work begins breaking them in and getting them riding and going. At the end of the year after being broken, they go to the trainer Dermot Weld.

The care and maintenance of thoroughbred horses is paramount. As Stan says, if there is good staff they will make good horses. There is the odd one that kicks the wall, but nervous horses are caused by nervous people around them.

Security at the stud is important, and things are less casual than they were in earlier times. A registered horse is no good once it is stolen, as was the case with Shergar. The thieves did not realise that the Aga Khan did not own the horse outright, but just had a few shares in the syndicate. In addition, a stolen horse cannot be registered, so it is of no use to anyone. Besides, horses know their own surroundings and become uneasy and difficult to handle when away from them.

Future of the Irish thoroughbred horse industry

Stan, who is a member of the Turf Club, has done some stewarding at various races. He says that the Turf Club is a great organisation because, with the exception of the Keeper of the Match Book and the office staff, all of the members work on a voluntary basis. So, if Stan is stewarding at the Galway races, for example, he gets nothing, not even expenses. There are four stewards per meeting, and if they were paid, it would become quite expensive. Stan also thinks it is a great idea to have the voluntary stewards because if they were paid, there would be a team going around the country and favouritism would probably creep in. The voluntary stewards are like the jury in a court case, he says, and the stipendiary steward tells them the rules, just as would a judge. He does not think that Horse Racing Ireland should do stewarding. This could become an issue, as the Minister for Agriculture can ask for a review of the board and business of Horse Racing Ireland. He firmly believes that the same body should not run everything involved in racing.

When asked about the success of the Irish horse racing industry, Stan is adamant that the Irish people's love of horses is a huge factor. He also points to Charlie McCreevy, former Minister for Finance, and Joe Walsh, former Minister for Agriculture, and believes that they were the saviours of Irish racing. They were both keen followers of horse racing, which showed when support was needed. Stan recalls that when the academy for training jockeys, RACE, started in 1972, Joe Walsh came to visit it at the very outset. He remembers the horse-owning syndicate named 'Tallaght Strategy' that was made up of members from several political parties. There is no fear of the future, he thinks, as at present some of the best trainers in Europe are in Ireland, as are the best horses, the best stallions, the best land with grass growing nearly ten months of the year, and, very importantly, the best personnel. Stan stresses the importance of personnel, because he says if someone loves horses, then that person is at one with the horse, and then there is a bond. He is strongly of the opinion that, "As long as Ireland is here and people are here, there'll be horse racing." ■

Presentation to the owner Oliver Murphy of Flutter Away, winner of the 1987 Moyglare Stud Stakes (Group 1) at the Curragh (ridden by Michael Kinane). Also in the photo are (left) Mary Weld, representing trainer Dermot Weld, and her son Mark, on far right is Peter Patrick Hemphill.

Tunney and his long-time assistant, Bob O'Brien, at the Listowel Races.

CHAPTER 6

TUNNEY GALVIN

" We used to get the results down from Limerick
from the Exchange Telegraph Company. You would ring up and
they would give you the results. "

Tunney Galvin's childhood and formative years were spent at 101 Rock Street, Tralee, where his family had a grocery business. In the year of Tunney's birth, his father John applied for a betting licence and set up a bookmaking business in Rock Street. The family, as was usual in those times, lived over the shop. Micheál and Seán were Tunney's elder brothers and he also had two sisters, Norrie and Mary. Norrie still continues the grocery business in Rock Street. Their mother was a Barrett, a relative of Austin Barrett, the Dublin bookmaker.

A strong sense of nationalism existed in Tralee at this time. Tunney remembers his father going to meetings of the Ancient Order of Hibernians, which were held near the Grafton Café, and this memory brings to mind the song 'A Nation Once Again', which Tunney recalls would always be sung by Ger Keeffe after an AOH meeting. Tunney was educated locally in Tralee completing his Intermediate Examination at CBS The Green in 1944. His father became ill around this time, and Tunney was required to manage his betting shop until his father's recovery.

Later he met his future wife, Áine Dineen, when delivering a copy of *The Greyhound Express* to John Chute's business premises where she was employed. She is a native of Rathmore, County Kerry, but in the Cork portion of the parish, she emphasises! Áine acknowledges that she knew nothing about racing when she first met her husband, but she assisted him once their seven children were reared.

Betting at the dogs

Tunney remembers the first meeting in the 1940s where he had his own pitch at Tralee greyhound track. There was considerable interest in greyhound betting, with meetings held twice a week in Tralee. He recalls occasions when there would regularly be twenty bookies, including local men such as Joe Sugrue and Gerry Moriarty. A bookmaker called Jim Clarke from Ballybunion regularly sent a Dubliner, Johnny Morgan, to represent him at the track. Significant money changed hands, particularly on Friday nights or on big race nights, and research into a dog's provenance was vital before offering odds.

The bookie's accoutrements for a meeting comprised a box to stand on, a slate to advertise the odds, his printed tickets and his betting bag. Tunney calls to mind local trainers such as Dan 'Sado' Walsh, Rory O'Connell and Dan Lynch, and his own brother, Fr Micheál, who was a successful trainer and who loved all sports.

Different times

In 1959, Tunney took over the building that had previously been used as the Post Office for his bookmaking business, and recalls Miss O'Brien, the famously strict postmistress. In those times there was no television or radio in the shop and very few people in Ireland had telephones, so bookmakers used the Exchange Telegraph Company to establish race results. This meant that hundreds of bookmakers would be ringing up the company in Limerick as this was the only means of getting race results before the following day's newspaper. Big horse races such as the English Grand National or Epsom Derby meant the betting shop would be full of punters, with the overflow moving into the grocery shop. The big Irish races were the Irish Grand National, the Irish Derby, the Galway Plate and some of the Curragh races such as 1,000 and 2,000 Guineas.

Tunney notes some Kerry men connected with thoroughbred racing, mentioning Dermot Whelehan and the jockey Bernard Dillon of Caherina, Tralee, who rode Lemberg in 1910, winning the Epsom Derby. Also, a horse named The Liberator, which was trained at Mounthawk in Tralee, won the 1879 Galway Plate.

Betting at the racecourse

Tunney can remember going to race meetings at Tralee racecourse in the 1930s when he was very young, at a time when the stand could not be used, he says, as it was unsafe. He credits James O'Hara, race secretary, for keeping the race meetings going at that time. He recalls that it was Tommy Sheehy, grandfather of journalist Pascal Sheehy, who looked after the course.

When Tunney began to undertake on-course betting, he operated at the races in Tralee, Killarney and Listowel. He had various clerks over the years, including Tommy McLaughlin, followed by Bob O'Brien, whom Tunney remembers as being very good with figures.

In order to get the most advantageous pitch, Tunney would arrive early, before the meeting opened to the public. He would study the racecard carefully but, as he says, he would only have a fleeting knowledge of the horses. The odds offered would be guided by a horse's known form. The business operated mostly in cash; during the bank strikes of 1966, 1970 and 1976, it was a predominantly cash business, with the consequent dangers of theft or a hold-up. Fortunately he was never to suffer either calamity.

He tells an anecdote about the wife of trainer Paddy Prendergast, who put each way bets on three runners, all of which won. This was during a bank strike and Tunney was asked to retain the money until the banks should open again. He declined, he says, as he had enough trouble looking after his own money!

Just like anyone in business, a bookmaker has to build up a reputation and credibility. Like most bookmakers in earlier times, Tunney relied on his own name as a sole trader, and he had his own clientèle. Naturally, a limit was put on bets, and he would have to act on his own initiative,

> ❝ You had to be good with figures, otherwise you weren't at the races. ❞

calculating his capacity to cover the bets before offering odds. This was quite stressful, as he had to be careful always not to go over the odds, since this could leave him with insufficient means left in the bag to pay out. As he remarks, it is "a quick cure for your carelessness" when you do not have sufficient money to pay out the bets.

There were no mobile phones then, and the bookie was dependent on public telephones which meant that long queues formed to get a call out. The betting started in earnest when the horses were called into the parade ring. Tunney eloquently describes the complexity of a bookmaker's business. He must focus very closely as he is trying to do several things at once: watch the other bookmakers and try to interpret the signals, calculate the odds, take in bets and give out betting slips in return. To be a bookie, Tunney says, you have to be good with figures and very quick and sharp. According to Gerry Rogers, a fellow bookmaker, a bookie has to be able to "mind mice at the crossroads".

A bookmaker might try various ploys to get in business, like setting a short price, which would start a charge of punters to his pitch. Although betting should be discontinued at the off, some bookies would continue taking bets.

Tunney has fond memories of some great characters among the bookies, such as Bill Quinlan and Malachy Skelly, the great banter amongst them all and the adrenalin and excitement of race meetings. He would stand on a box all day but, as he says, that did not bother him once he was busy. He was using his mind all the time, joshing with the punters and other bookies and calculating odds.

Tunney remarks philosophically that time and tide wait for no man, and times have certainly changed. He recalls going to the Curragh and returning home again on £10 of petrol! He reflects on his favourite racecourses over the years and has fond memories of Listowel, a great meeting place, where he had a large clientèle, and of Galway which was also very good for business. Áine usually did not travel to the racecourses but would sometimes go with Tunney to Punchestown or the Galway festival, where they would take an apartment for the duration.

He feels that the business gave him and his family a good living, and as Áine says with a smile, they reared seven children and had dinner every day. Tunney remarks that it is very important to develop the right attitude to life, whatever your occupation. ■

Tunney Galvin lunching with his children in 1985 at the Listowel Races.

Bookmaker Tunney Galvin.

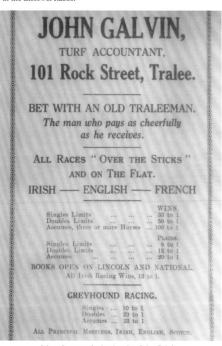

JOHN GALVIN,
TURF ACCOUNTANT,
101 Rock Street, Tralee.

BET WITH AN OLD TRALEEMAN.
*The man who pays as cheerfully
as he receives.*

ALL RACES " OVER THE STICKS "
AND ON THE FLAT.

IRISH —— ENGLISH —— FRENCH

				WINS.
Singles Limits	...	...	...	33 to 1
Doubles Limits	...	...	...	50 to 1
Accumes, three or more Horses	...	100 to 1
				PLACES.
Singles Limits	...	...	...	8 to 1
Doubles Limits	...	...	...	12 to 1
Accumes	...	...	...	20 to 1

BOOKS OPEN ON LINCOLN AND NATIONAL.
All Irish Racing Wins, 12 to 1.

GREYHOUND RACING.

Singles	...	10 to 1
Doubles	...	20 to 1
Accumes	...	33 to 1

ALL PRINCIPAL MEETINGS, IRISH, ENGLISH, SCOTCH.

Advertisement for bookmaker John Galvin,
101 Rock Street, Tralee, in the 1920s.

Norman Colfer during his time in Kells, Co. Meath.

CHAPTER 7

NORMAN COLFER

" We had all sorts of well-known people.
Robert Sangster was the man at the time, and he was buying
everything around him. It was quite exciting. "

PROFILE

Norman Colfer

**Ratoath
Co. Meath**

Born:
1928

Occupation:
**Auctioneer
and racecourse
manager**

Auctioneer and racecourse manager Norman Colfer comes from New Ross, County Wexford. His father and grandfather were in the legal profession, and following his early education at Glenstal, Norman read law at Trinity College, Dublin.

Norman's father was honorary secretary of the Wexford Hounds for over thirty years, and his mother, Eileen Walsh, was a keen horse-woman, who showed horses and competed in point to points. Norman understands that his mother rode in the first ever ladies' point to point in Ireland. This tradition of horsemanship continues, and Norman's niece is now chairman of the Wexford Hounds. He did ride himself but only during the holidays; he claims to be a "very bad shot, a middling fisherman and a poor golfer"!

In an interesting historical aside, Norman's family had a shareholding in Cherry's Brewery, which Guinness took over in the 1950s in order to obtain a brewing licence in Ireland.

Auctioneering

Norman recalls travelling to auctions as a boy with his mother, and being absolutely fascinated by the man who wielded the gavel. This was his first introduction to the world of auctioneering.

He explains that it was understood that he would go for the Bar, having been taught debating at Glenstal. However, the years during which a new barrister can spend waiting around for briefs were less than attractive to young Norman. Following a short period of study at TCD, he changed direction, and in 1948 he became an apprentice auctioneer at the firm of Smith Griffin (later Osborne King Megran) at 64 Dawson Street, Dublin. There he paid his fee and underwent his three-year apprenticeship with Willie Smith, undertaking office duties, showing houses to potential buyers, clerking at the auctions, hiring porters, preparing catalogues and so on. Norman remembers that not long after he started, he was conducting auctions himself, and for each of these he was paid £3 in addition to his weekly wage of £1. He recalls that a lot of house contents were being sold during this time, and there were also many property sales.

Then in 1954, a solicitor in Kells who was a friend contacted him to say that a job was to be advertised in *The Irish Times* and if he applied for it, he would get it. Norman duly applied and, in his mid 20s, found himself working for J. C. Brady in Kells, County Meath, running the cattle sales yard and auctioning cattle. Mr Brady also had several other yards in Meath and Cavan. Sometime later, he and Norman parted ways, and Mr Brady passed away soon afterwards.

Norman then became a freelance auctioneer, a profession in which he has continued until quite recently. As he says, auctioneering is either something that comes naturally to a person or it does not. His reputation as an auctioneer was building, and four or five days a week he sold cattle at marts all over Ireland. He considers himself fortunate to have worked with two highly effective auctioneers at Smith Griffin, and to have learned a lot while working as a clerk. There is a technique and skill in working the crowd, he says, and the essence of the auctioneer's skill is that he has to figure out who is buying, and at what price level.

Norman was now married to Vera Heywood Jones, and they had a family. Vera's English father was a very charming and decent man, Norman remarks. He worked for some time with Seamus McGrath, a horse trainer in Glencairn, and he also rode very well. Sadly, in 1981 Vera passed away. Norman married Ann Brownlow in 1984.

Norman was always keen on racing and on his day off on Saturdays, he would go with his friends to any race meeting that was held, and he became familiar with many people at the various racecourses. He admits to being a bad gambler because he followed the money, which he says one should never do!

Fairyhouse

In 1968, an advertisement appeared for the position of manager of Fairyhouse racecourse in Ratoath, County Meath. Patrick Reeves Smith who was manager at the time and a good friend, was also Secretary of the Association of Irish Racecourses. Norman decided to apply for the position and was called for interview on his fortieth birthday. He remembers that George Malcolmson chaired the panel of four interviewers. Following the interview nothing transpired until, after a cattle market some time later, he heard that a man had been asking about him. Two weeks later he received a letter asking him to meet Mr Malcolmson and Standish Collen, who offered him the position of part-time manager of Fairyhouse Racecourse on a salary of £1,000 a year. Norman accepted and he was to remain in this post for the next twenty years.

His only knowledge of Fairyhouse came from his attendance as a race goer. He was fortunate that a good foreman, John McCarthy, had been working in Fairyhouse for many years, and Norman realised that as long as he had John on his side, everything would work out. Also, his friends rallied round, such as former manager Patrick Reeves Smith, who was available for a time to teach him the ropes, and Peter Martin who was running Punchestown at this time. However, he found that he still had to do all the administrative work, as no secretary was available, so he bought a typewriter. While previously he had only been able to go racing on Saturdays, now, for the first time, he watched the Grand National live on a Monday, and it was he who was running the racecourse! He remembers the event as a great start to his career at Fairyhouse, with about 25,000 people at the races on one day.

Naturally, making the racecourse self-sufficient was crucial to its success; it was imperative to find sources of income and Norman began to seek sponsorship. He recalls an unexpected event. Shortly after he became manager of Fairyhouse, he had a visit from Captain Spencer Freeman of the Irish Hospitals Sweepstake company. Rumours had circulated of a Sweeps hurdle being run at Leopardstown, but rebuilding work was being undertaken there so it was likely that this race meeting would either go to Punchestown or to Fairyhouse. When Captain Freeman asked Norman why the Sweeps race should be given to Fairyhouse, Norman replied "Because we need the money, sir!" The deal was done – simple as that! Fairyhouse already had sponsorship with the Powers Gold Cup, the Jameson stand and the Irish Distillers Grand National race, but there were only fifteen race meetings a year and all income had to be generated on those particular days. The racecourse company was not master of its own destiny, as it did not own the stands and the avenue. This was owned by landlord John Caule, and latterly his widow, though fortunately the company was in a position to buy the land later.

Fairyhouse was a National Hunt meeting which had evolved from the Ward Union Hunt. The Irish Grand National was run annually on Easter Monday – a public holiday. Norman recalls that in those days, bank holidays affected only bank staff so, luckily for management, it was not necessary to pay overtime or extra allowances to staff at the racecourse. When Baldoyle racecourse closed, the race meeting previously held there on January 1st became available. Norman advised the board to apply for this date, which was duly done, and it became the most successful date on the Fairyhouse calendar after Easter Monday,

Another source of income for racecourses was from car parking. Norman says that the Racing Board had bought out the rights for this at a number of racecourses, but not at Fairyhouse, Galway, Leopardstown and Punchestown, because they were too expensive to buy out. This income was incredibly useful, as on an average Easter Monday, the car parks might take in about £3,000, a considerable amount at that time. This situation was later to change, when orthodox business methods were applied in order to cut out the car park fee collectors. Car parking became free, resulting in a loss of earnings to the racecourse, and as a result the prices at the stiles increased. Galway continued to charge and derived a large income from the car parks. There were no television rights in those days, and a racecourse had to make its money on the gate. However, there was always a large attendance because race meetings were major events on the social calendar.

A good horse would always help to draw the crowds, and Norman remembers that the Dreapers and the Moores always had good horses. He also gives credit to the excellent fencemen who worked at Fairyhouse such as Jimmy Woods and Kevin Derby, who skilfully constructed the birch and gorse fences. A further attraction at Fairyhouse was the introduction of larger prize money, such as the Irish Sweeps Hurdle in the late 1960s, the announcement of which by Charles J. Haughey at the Gresham Hotel is recalled. Subsequently, in 1995, Mr Haughey's horse, Flashing Steel, won the Irish Grand National, trained by his son-in-law, John Mulhern.

In those times, conditions at Fairyhouse racecourse were somewhat primitive. Norman's office was comprised of a desk, two chairs and a counter. Also, the stand was becoming unstable to the extent that when an aeroplane flew low over it, the foundations would shake. This never stopped Norman climbing to the top to get the best view of the races! He remarks that the people who worked there knew the place, and had a real love for it. However, times were changing, and in the late 1980s the corporate concept was evolving, and although he accepts that change is inevitable, it did not suit Norman. He preferred the ordinary punter who came on the wet Wednesday and not the group who only came occasionally, such as on festival days.

> " When an aeroplane flew low over the stand at
> Fairyhouse, the foundations would shake! "

The Association of Irish Racecourses

Norman Colfer describes the Association of Irish Racecourses (AIR) as an unofficial trade association. The original chairman was Andrew Moore, of the Macardle Moore Brewery in Dundalk, and the AIR began as a group of Irish racecourses, apart from Leopardstown, which was run by the Racing Board, and the Curragh, run by the Turf Club. Norman feels that initially these two racecourses felt that the others were against them, as these bodies exercised control over certain elements of racing. For example, he recalls the price of a racecard being controlled at sixpence, though it cost him the same to produce it, so there was no profit to be made. Similarly, the Racing Board controlled the Tote which was very important to the racecourses. Incidentally, Norman points out that the first Tote ever run was at Fairyhouse.

The Association of Irish Racecourses was regarded by the Racing Board and the Turf Club as being bold and daring. However, with the introduction of television rights and the deal struck by the AIR, feelings changed, and the Racing Board and Turf Club "got fond of them", Norman says. Norman recalls that when he became involved with the AIR, Patrick Reeves Smith was the

Norman Colfer. *The Irish Field. Photograph Frank Fennell.*

Rossberbon, the Colfer home in New Ross, Co. Wexford, where Norman grew up.

Norman Colfer.

Norman Colfer at the desk during a sale.

secretary and, at each meeting a racecourse representative was present, usually the manager and perhaps a colleague. There were perhaps twenty people at a meeting. When the AIR was expanding, it became necessary to employ a full-time manager. As an example of the complexity of such an organisation, Norman says that when a race meeting was being arranged, he had to contact Timmy Murphy to organise "the Dublin staff", who sold the race cards, manned the stiles and so on. However, the "Dublin staff" formed a union, and one year they went on strike for increased wages and overtime, three days before the Grand National. This was the type of challenge that the AIR had to overcome.

In time, the presiding secretary of the AIR left the job, and Norman took on the role during the chairmanship of Conor O'Hagan. Gilbert Barrington, who ran Roscommon racecourse and was also an accountant with a practice in Dublin, was a member of the AIR, and Norman remembers him as a brilliant and astute man. The entire income-generating element of racecourses now changed when Satellite Information Services (SIS) entered the scene. Norman recalls meeting, together with Conor O'Hagan and Gilbert Barrington, with a intelligent Englishman from SIS, who proposed buying television rights to Irish racecourses, a process which was already being undertaken on English racecourses. Prior to this, only an audio commentary was undertaken at Irish racecourses. As Norman recalls, SIS made a very good offer which was accepted. However, the decision was not popular in the media, and he remembers the AIR receiving terrible abuse from the newspapers about the deal! Nevertheless, the arrangement has stood the test of time, with increased income every year – the racecourses are getting money for nothing since 1994, he says. He credits Conor and Gilbert for the success of this deal, as it has made the racecourses almost independent of the Racing Board and the Turf Club. Part of the original deal was that all courses or races would be equal, thus the status of Laytown would be the same as that of the Curragh. In Norman's view, this is what has kept the small race tracks alive through difficult times. In addition, once the first race has started, the racecourse is guaranteed its money, and he says it would hard for a business to make a mess of that.

In 1992 Norman was made a member of the Irish National Hunt Steeplechase Committee and he was elected in 1997 to the Turf Club. He has acted as steward at race meetings in Ulster and Leinster.

Selling at Goffs and Windsor Car Sales

Since his days with J. C. Brady in Kells, Norman had worked as a freelance auctioneer and so he worked with various auction houses around the country. He reflects on being twice employed and let go by Goffs! Originally Goffs operated in Ballsbridge, in the sales paddocks opposite the RDS. The firm then moved to Kill, with financial support from Paddy McGrath and others, and a good operation was built there which has been very successful.

At this time, Norman was working at marts around the country selling cattle together with Sir Peter Nugent, a friend who was also an auctioneer. Norman says that Peter was very good with the farmers; he was also running a stud near Clane. Norman recalls that although they both worked hard every day, they never had any money! Then Goffs advertised for auctioneers;

Norman was interviewed and got the job, which at £1,500 a year was quite a good salary compared to his earnings from some of his other endeavours. He remembers Goffs as being an amazing establishment, nothing like he had ever known before. He describes the horse owners there as very different to those who are selling at other auctions or sales. The auctioneer assesses a horse's worth before the sale and, in Norman's opinion, a horse is worth what his sire was worth. However, this tends not to be the view of the sellers; huge reserves were put on horses for sale, and people would get others to put in bids in order to inflate the values. Unfortunately, after a time, his employment there was brought to an end, for reasons he has never understood. Perhaps, as they said, he spoke too quickly, or perhaps it was because he was not grand enough, or they had someone else in mind, or he was selling too quickly, rather than trying to "squeeze more out of the one buyer on the floor", as he puts it.

Norman had not enjoyed selling at Goffs at this time, as the system there was to roster fifteen horses to an auctioneer at a time. He felt he could not get "heated up" and get the crowd going. In any case, Norman made his first exit from Goffs.

About two years later, Goffs again advertised for auctioneers. Norman asked a friend to determine whether he should apply and, when the response was positive, he did so and was successful at interview. However, after a time he was once again let go and told "You need not come back", without further explanation. In his opinion, Goffs was controlled by the top people in the industry. As there was no contract, he was a free agent.

In 1974, during a break when selling cattle in Kingscourt, County Cavan, Michael O'Reilly approached Norman about auctioning cars. This gentleman, together with a partner, had bought a garage in Rialto in Dublin, and because trade was poor, they had devised a plan to auction cars. Norman agreed to go with Michael to London the following Tuesday to be present at a car auction at Alexandra Palace. A month later, Windsor Car Auctions held a hugely successful car auction in a pub in Harold's Cross in Dublin with Norman as auctioneer, at which 77 out of 80 cars were sold. A short time later, a car dealer's business in Kilkenny failed, and the accountant there knew Michael O'Reilly, and offered him 200 cars for sale. Michael decided to sell twenty cars a week over ten weeks, which marked the start of a very successful business. This business later became Merlin Car Auctions, and Norman continued working with the business for thirty-seven years. ■

Jockey Phonsie O'Brien in his heyday.

CHAPTER 8

PHONSIE O'BRIEN

" We had the natural knowledge from our father on how to manage horses properly. I rode great horses, and horses that were schooled to perfection. "

Phonsie O'Brien's father Dan was a farmer in Churchtown, County Cork. He also bought and sold horses and was very keen on racing. Dan was an only son, and had five sisters all of whom entered religious life and worked in the USA. Phonsie recalls that he learned to ride at the age of seven or eight, and that his father bought him a pony, "and a difficult little pony he was!" As a child, Phonsie attended the local national school and, when he was eight or nine, attended the Dominican preparatory school in Wicklow as a boarder. Later, he received his secondary education at Rockwell College. His father Dan had married twice, and Donal, the eldest son of his first marriage, was bequeathed the family farm; Vincent, Pauline, Dermot and Phonsie were the children of his second marriage. He remarks that his father always had a good pony for him, which meant that when he went hunting with the Duhallow Hounds, he would lead the hunt. Hunting was wonderful training for both the horse and the rider, he says.

Ballydoyle

On completion of his secondary education, he began working for his brother Vincent, who was renting the farm from their half-brother Donal, and training horses. Phonsie recalls that Vincent's best early client was Frank Vickerman, who owned Cottage Rake which became only the first horse to win the Cheltenham Gold Cup three years in a row, from 1948 to 1950. Vincent O'Brien had no land of his own, and he decided the time had come to buy his own property. As Phonsie recalls, Vincent went about this by playing poker several nights a week and, being an astute gambler, he won much of the time! By the late 1940s, when he had amassed almost £20,000, he and Phonsie began to view properties. Once they saw Ballydoyle, near Cashel, they knew that this was the place they wanted. Ballydoyle's previous owner was a Mr Sadler, a wealthy bookmaker from London. Vincent moved his stable of horses from Churchtown, and set up an effective working partnership with this brothers Phonsie and Dermot, who had just left the Irish Army.

At this time, at the December Newmarket sales, Vincent had spoken with Sam Armstrong about the possibility of Phonsie riding for him, and an arrangement had been made that he would start working for Armstrong the following April, which was, in fact, never to happen. In the interim, Phonsie rode in a number of races for Vincent and, as he remarks: "that was the end of Newmarket"! His first winner was in a bumper at Limerick Junction on Burton Wood, owned by Mrs Townsend and, for a further four years, Phonsie rode for Vincent as an amateur jockey. In those days, an amateur was restricted to riding a limited number of races, because of possible complaints from professional jockeys, but Phonsie secured permission to ride Vincent's horses exclusively.

Phonsie was fortunate in his career to have avoided serious injury or major accidents; he believes that he had a natural skill to ride jump horses, although, being of a large build, he had to be careful with his weight. He remembers that when he left school, his weight was 12 stone 3 pounds; for riding as an amateur he could reduce this to 10 stone 9 pounds. The day he rode in the Grand National on Royal Tan, he was 10 stone 3 pounds, but it was not possible for him to maintain this weight. He twice came second in the Aintree Grand National on Royal Tan. He always followed Vincent's instructions to the letter, he says. Vincent disapproved of overuse of the whip, maintaining that if a horse had the ability to win, it would do so. Phonsie says that he never stopped a horse.

Knock Hard, trained by Vincent O'Brien, won the Cheltenham Gold Cup in 1953, and when he had a win with Cottage Rake, the real beginning of his success as a trainer was marked. In Phonsie's opinion, a whole new era in horse racing was ushered in. He believes that this success was due to the expertise and experience of the staff, a natural knowledge derived from Dan O'Brien on how to manage horses, and most importantly, some good owners. He is emphatic that good owners bring good horses to a trainer. He also reflects on the fact that some trainers at the time resented Vincent's success.

The working day at Ballydoyle

Phonsie recalls that the Ballydoyle day began at 7 a.m. with breakfast for the staff, with the horses being ridden out at 8 a.m. Unlike other yards, the men had breakfast before work, and afterwards would ride the horses out until lunchtime, depending on the number of horses. He explains that Vincent worked to a strict discipline, and was meticulous in schooling the horses to perfection. His policy was not to work the horses too hard, with the longest distance set at one or one and half miles, galloping at speed. Phonsie and Danny O'Sullivan rode the jumping horses in pairs, riding eight horses over sixteen jumps on Tuesdays and Fridays each week. Phonsie stresses the importance of having an empathetic relationship with the person jumping with you, in order that each would not upset the other.

Phonsie has fond memories of the Tralee races, and he remarks that it was one of his favourite meetings in the 1950s and 1960s, and he also recalls the old-world Benner's Hotel in the town. His elder brother, Dermot, while stationed in army barracks in Kerry, was also particularly fond of Benner's. Other favourite racecourses that come to his mind are Leopardstown, Limerick Junction and Mallow, which had "good layouts and cambers on the bends which make them lovely racetracks to go around".

Phonsie retired as a jockey around 1953 and, in the mid-1950s, he began training horses, which he continued to do until 2006. He reflects on the fact that in his lifetime he has worked only for his family and for himself, which suited him as he always wished to be independent. He recalls that, at one time, he had a bank loan on which 17% interest was being charged. He managed to pay off that debt in two or three years, and since then he is happy to say that he has had no loans.

Reflecting on his life and that of his brother, Phonsie believes that he and Vincent were alike in that they sought always for perfection in their work. They were fortunate in having a sense of vision, and could understand the potential of something, be it a property or a horse. In personality, however, they differed; Phonsie remembers Vincent as a quiet, introverted man who was secure in himself, while he himself was always far more extrovert by nature.

South Lodge and Thomastown

Phonsie O'Brien bought South Lodge from Major Douglas for £9,300 in the late 1940s. This was a very good buy as the Major had just undertaken work on the roof, he says. Phonsie improved the property by adding new gallops and stables, but however, about nine years later, he sold it in a poker game for £125,000, to the serious displeasure of his wife, Anne! Anne O'Brien née Pilsworth, is one of the the milling family of Thomastown, County Kilkenny. Then Phonsie bought part of the estate around Thomastown Castle, near Golden, County Tipperary, and he built a house, gallops and American-style stables there. Robert Sangster and Vincent O'Brien were so impressed with his improvements at Thomastown that they wanted to buy the property, Phonsie recalls. After about ten years, he sold this property for about £1,000,000 and then moved to his present home at Landscape House.

Phonsie and Anne O'Brien have three daughters; Gillian, who worked with her father for a time but now works in bone treatment for horses; Yvonne, who is married to Adrian Nicoll, chairman of BBA Ireland and involved with bloodstock sales and purchases; and Mary Ann, who is founder and managing director of Lily O'Briens Chocolates and is married to Jonathan Irwin, formerly of Goffs.

Phonsie has trained horses for Michael Sheehan, at one time the Lord Mayor of Cork, and John A. Wood, who was his main client for whom he trained six or eight jumpers. He remembers Mr Wood as a very pleasant man, with whom he got on very well.

Back in the 1950s, the thoroughbred business was not well established in Ireland. Horses were sent to England occasionally and Vincent O'Brien was the first trainer to send a horse to the USA. This was Sir Ivor owned by the American Ambassador to Ireland, Raymond R. Guest, which won the Washington DC International Stakes at Laurel Park, Maryland, in 1968. This win was the cause of major celebration for the O'Briens. Phonsie recalls that Mr Guest had to listen to the results of the race on the radio, because he was on ambassadorial duties that day in County Wicklow. Sir Ivor was a marvellous horse, and he was also the winner of the 1968 Epsom Derby.

The business of training

Phonsie discusses the importance of having good owners and of building up a good relationship with people. He had three or four American owners, but had only 25 or 30 horses at a time, in the interests of keeping the business small and exclusive. Through his brother Vincent, he was given a number of horses to be trained for Marlon Kline of the pharmaceutical company Smith Kline & French. This proved to be a crucial contact for Phonsie, as Kline's relative, Miles Valentine and his wife Joy, became Phonsie's main owners for about sixteen years, with considerable success. Phonsie says that he was a close friend of Robert Sangster; he trained a number of horses for him and always accompanied him when he was buying horses.

> " I was to start work for Sam Armstrong in Newmarket in April. In the meantime, I rode in a number of races for Vincent, and that was the end of Newmarket! "

He recalls his staff with pride, while admitting that he was a strict employer who insisted they conform to the correct methods. He remembers Johnny Brabston and headman Willie O'Brien, who, he says, produced the best turned out horses for any race in Ireland or Britain. He is adamant that good staff and riders make the work worthwhile. His jockeys included the great Bobby Beasley and Stan Mellor, who rode his winners at the Galway Plate.

When asked about changes in horse racing, Phonsie comments that the earlier system needed quite a bit of change, and he maintains that such changes are for the good of horse racing. He describes Denis Brosnan as being very effective in his role as chairman of Horse Racing Ireland, and a man who has made a significant difference in the area of the financing of racing.

Phonsie says horse racing is a business where one succeeds or fails – there is no middle ground. Trainers need owners, so the quality must be maintained to get the owners interested. Throughout his career, he has been fortunate in that he was able to depend upon himself and his own resources for the majority of the time. He keeps careful account of the financial side of the business, and, as he says, from being a man with no "acre of land", he has turned his fortunes around. He recalls his brother Vincent saying that you make your own luck, but you need 5% or 10% extra luck in addition to all the hard work! ∎

The O'Brien brothers: Vincent, Dermot and Phonsie, with the young Anthony Fogarty looking on, at the Killarney races. *The Cork Examiner.*

Cottage Rake with jockey Aubrey Brabazon in the Curragh racecourse yard in 1947, with Vincent O'Brien looking on.

Phonsie O'Brien.

Monk's Star with jockey Francis Flood, led by Patrick Joyce, from Paddy Sleator's yard. Photograph courtesy of Betty Galway-Greer.

CHAPTER 9

FRANCIS FLOOD

" Starter Major Scott used to say that
the ones that want to start will be up in front, and the ones
that don't will be at the back. "

F rancis Flood grew up in Grange Con Rocks, County Wicklow, close to Counties Carlow and Kildare. His father, Tom, worked for the Irish Land Commission and also had a farm. He kept a couple of horses, and generally ran one at Punchestown, though incredibly, he never sat on a horse himself. Sadly, he did not live to see his son's great success, passing away before he reached the age of 60. Francis recalls Paddy Powell senior, a top Flat jockey who worked with Tom for a few years. He rode in many races in England, and rode Easter Hero, a top chaser who fell in the Grand National, bringing down most the field.

Francis was the second youngest of eleven children, and he remembers his childhood as being happy, though times were tough. He remarks that he was never fond of the farm, and so when he was about 17 or 18, he began work for Paddy Sleator, who was a local horse trainer at nearby Grange Con Stables, and a friend of his father. Francis, with his wife Teresa, has lived at Ballynure since the late 1960s, not far from his home place. Today, his son is also working in the business with him.

Amateur jockey

It was when he started at Paddy Sleator's that Francis really learned how to ride. At the time, in the late 1940s, he was fortunate to get a job, he says. He started to ride out on the quiet horses, and slowly his skill improved. He also helped out with the stables. Then he got a lucky break, winning a race at Killarney, and the following week he rode two other winners.

He was lucky to ride some good horses such as Another Flash which won the Champion Hurdle. Paddy Sleator was not a difficult man to work for, and Francis explains that he was dedicated to training horses, was very meticulous, and believed that it was important that he got the best out of a horse.

Francis rode mainly in bumpers, which are the National Hunt flat races, and also in the occasional hurdle or chase. He was never afraid of jumping, however, and he remembers that he was started off on an experienced horse, which built up your confidence. In addition, he did a lot of hunting and rode in point to point races all over the country, but he did not travel as much as amateurs do today. In any case, he says, Paddy Sleator did not encourage him to do so as he did not want him to get injured.

At that time, the professional jockeys were not making a good living. Naturally, they would not be happy if amateurs took rides from them, especially in the jump races, as they would then lose their fee. Francis says that an amateur jockey might get away with doing four or five jump races a year but not more than that. A National Hunt jockey would have the choice of working as an amateur or a professional, and if an amateur rode too often in the jump races then he would be banned.

He recalls that at that time, the horses would travel to the races in a CIÉ horsebox, and he himself would travel with Paddy Sleator in his car. Paddy rarely stayed overnight at the races, except at Killarney where he might stay a few nights, and if so, Francis would make his own way home.

As an amateur jockey, Francis rarely got money for winning. The prize money for races was small, but often an owner would bet for you and that was the way you would be compensated for your expenses and so on. He never wanted to leave Paddy's yard, or to turn professional, for several reasons. He explains that he always had the best horses there, and did not think that he could improve his situation by going somewhere else. In addition, with regard to weight, the lowest weight for National Hunt races was around 11 stone, which was fine for him, and he would have struggled to make 10 stone 5 or 6 pounds, which was the weight he would have had to maintain if he turned professional. He recalls the other jockeys who worked for Paddy over the years, including Bobby Beasley, who later did very well in England, Tony Prendergast, Paddy Powell and Noel Sleator, who was Paddy Sleator's cousin.

Many changes have come about since his time as a jockey, and these include the wearing of back protectors and helmets. Neither back protectors or helmets were worn for riding over fences and hurdles, or on the Flat. The starting line was a tape, and now starting stalls are in use. Francis describes Major Scott as a very good starter, who believed that the ones who wanted to start would be up at the front, and the ones that did not would be at back, so he allowed the jockeys to sort themselves out. As Francis puts it, if a jockey fancied himself, he would make sure that he was in the best position at the starting line.

Francis does not recall any interference from another rider during a race. He does not remember making much use of the whip, but he acknowledges that sometimes one would get carried away in the moment and over-use it. There were no penalties in earlier times, but nowadays the race is watched back on film, and the stewards will spot issues which need to be addressed. Also, in former times, there was no photo finish. He explains that sometimes there was a difference of opinion as to who had won a race, but it did not happen very often. As a jockey, once you had passed the finishing post, your job was done.

He remembers Punchestown as a place where he won every race once as a jockey, and some perhaps two or three times. His favourite race tracks were Leopardstown and Punchestown, and he rode five winners one year at Punchestown and four in another. The great thing about Punchestown in his day, he says, is that most of the horses were owned by farmers, and all of Ireland would be represented for those two days in the year. It was very popular and had a wonderful atmosphere.

He also rode a couple of winners at the Phoenix Park racecourse, which he describes as a very good Flat track, though the bends were a bit tight in the jumping races. Phoenix Park was very popular at show weeks in August, and the Saturday meets were also very well attended. He had a few winners at Tralee, both in riding and training, and he says that this was the best track of the three Kerry meetings, although he acknowledges that Killarney has improved a lot. He remembers that Tralee was a "right good galloping track" with a great run home on a climb of five furlongs that a good horse such as Dawn Run could win. He is sorry to see any racecourse close down, as Tralee has been forced to do. In Francis's days as a jockey, he remembers stewarding as being good, and he recalls some very smart stipendiary stewards like Jim Marsh and a few others.

Francis assures us that he did not have a following; it was more the horse that would be followed! He remembers Martin Molony and Aubrey Brabazon as two of his favourite jockeys. Once a race is won, it is great to know that the owner, in particular, is pleased. "That's the real kick", he says. There are some fantastic owners that really enjoy the racing, and that makes all the hard work worthwhile.

He was very fortunate never to have had a serious fall. He certainly broke a few bones, including his collar-bone, but nothing serious happened during his twenty years of riding. Even before he retired from jockeying, Francis was training for a few owners, and they were nervous about accidents, because if he was hurt, who then would train their horses?

Trainer

When Francis was growing up, the family did not own a horse, and as has been stated, he worked initially at Grange Con and then moved to nearby Ballynure. He bought a mare and won a couple of races with her. She bred a horse called Garoupe, which he trained. This horse was run at Cheltenham, but was a faller at the last fence. She won the Irish National at Fairyhouse in 1970 with Cathal Finnegan on board, and second in that race was another horse trained by Francis – Glencaraig Lady.

On a visit from England, George Owen, who had trained two Grand National winners, had bought Garoupe as a foal, which he left with Francis to train to run in bumpers. With Francis on board, the horse ran at Punchestown and won. This was fantastic, as the owner, Mrs Francis Williams, and her husband attended the race meeting. The horse was left with Francis and he went on to win the Irish Grand National in 1970.

Glencaraig Lady, owned by P. Doyle, had already run twice at Cheltenham before winning the Gold Cup in 1972. In 1970 she had fallen at the last fence and in 1971 she fell at the third last fence. Francis remembers her as being difficult to train. Frank Berry rode for the first time at Cheltenham on Glencaraig Lady in 1972, and he was up against all the top horses and trainers.

Great success was achieved with the horses owned by Mick Foster and Tony Allen, the musical duo. Francis was given a budget of £12,000 to buy a horse, and he went off to the sales and saw Nancy Myles. He had decided to offer £5,000 for her, but a friend discovered that the reserve

> " Paddy Sleator was a really dedicated man who thought of nothing but training horses. That was his life. "

was £4,500, so Francis offered that and got her. She was a beautiful chestnut that won nineteen races and made quite a lot of money when she went out to stud. As Francis says, Foster and Allen were very lucky people all their lives, and they had great success with one or two horses.

At one time, Francis was asked by Mick Holly, one of his owners, to buy a horse to be raffled for the GAA. Liam O'Flaherty, the Kerry footballer won that particular horse. Francis was later asked to buy another horse to be raffled which he did. The name of this horse was Ross Beigh Creek and the new owner following this raffle was Hugh Ferguson.

Francis's owners over the years included Bob Kelsey from Northern Ireland. He owned Bobsline, a jumper, which won twenty-six races, including the Arkle Trophy in 1984 at Cheltenham with Frank Berry riding. At one stage, Bobsline won ten or eleven races in a row before being beaten.

Another horse that he recalls is Feathered Friend, owned by Tom Wright and Michael Ahern from Dublin, which won the Kerry National at Listowel in 1982. More recently Francis trained G V A Ireland, owned by the late Donal Ó Buachalla, which won the John Smith's Midlands Grand National in 2006 at Uttoxeter with Ruby Walsh on board.

Mrs Teresa Flood (left), F. J. Flood (jockey), owner Dudley Sanger, Frank O'Reilly, chairman of Punchestown racecourse, and trainer Francis Flood, on the occasion when Whip Along won the Conyngham Cup Chase in 1990.

Francis Flood.

Trainer Francis Flood (left) and his wife, Teresa, with owner Mrs Urquahart (second right) receiving trophy.

Frank Berry on board Glencaraig Lady, trained by Francis Flood, winning the 1972 Cheltenham Gold Cup Steeplechase.

A trainer needs good land with a good hill which helps to keep the horses sound, Francis explains. Before nuts were introduced, the feed was a mash which included oats, flaxseed and bran. The life of a trainer, he says, involves long hours and hard work, but you know what you're doing, you have to be able to cope. He always understood horses pretty well, but as to whether he is a good judge of a horse, he admits that he did buy some which were good value, but he also bought some duds. A good trainer requires patience and time, and he must have knowledge of a horse in order to understand how much work it can take, and to recognise whether it is in form or not. A horse always looks forward to a break in the summer. If a horse is over-raced, it gets sour and does not want to race. Francis feels that it is a great help to be born into the racing world.

Francis is not much of a betting man, and says that he would not get carried away with the betting. There is so much competition now, the odds are not good. He feels that it is hard to compete with the French horses being brought here by some trainers over the last four or five years. These horses have a good record in France before they come here, and thus they are, in fact, he says "almost readymade winners". He agrees that in Ireland there are certainly good top class hurdlers and chasers, and that bodes well for the future.

Looking back today, Francis Flood declares that it is hard to describe how different things were during the time he was with Paddy Sleator. There were not so many trainers then and less competition. The people who had the money to spend were able to get the best horses. "The small lad", he says, would get a chance in those days, but then the money was not there in the same way. If owners had to sell because they needed the cash, then buyers would get good value, but it is very difficult to get good value in buying a horse today. The sport is now dominated by very wealthy owners who are able to buy top horses.

Francis likes to use jockeys Barry Geraghty and Mark Walsh, and he says that he might give rides to some of the lads in the yard. He likes to give support to local talent such as Denis O'Regan, who rode his first winner with Francis, and is now doing quite well in England.

Francis Flood has enjoyed his life, and he feels that he has learned an awful lot. He maintains his great interest in horses, and, health permitting, is still up early each morning, working with his son "because [he says] you have to get up when you have responsibilities". Naturally, he would like a few "top ones" but they do not come along very often, and he declares that the people he enjoys training for are the people who really enjoy their tracing. ■

Francis on board Bobsline (left), trained by Bob Casey.

Place d'Étoile winning the Pretty Polly Stakes at the Curragh, 1970.

CHAPTER 10

CHRISTOPHER
GAISFORD-ST LAWRENCE

❝ When I joined the Turf Club, it was too Anglo
(for want of a better word). The new modern Irishman with a bit of
money wasn't there. **❞**

A keen racegoer, Christopher Gaisford-St Lawrence was invited to join the Turf Club in 1970. Prior to this he had been a steward at Baldoyle and Phoenix Park racecourses. Baldoyle was his local track and he recalls its closure in 1973. The stands had been in poor structural condition and were close to being uninsurable, he says. At this time, the course and stands at Leopardstown were being rebuilt and the racing authorities were keen to transfer the racing days from Baldoyle. All in all, it had become uneconomic for Baldoyle to remain open.

Christopher has owned racehorses since the late 1960s when he bought two yearlings, one of which went on to be quite successful. During the 1970s he had about six two- and three-year old horses a year in training, and he and his wife Penelope had about fifty winners over the years. He explains that like most small owners he had horses for the enjoyment of racing, and, of course, in the hope of winning. He considers it ridiculous to talk of a horse racing industry. Owners in the majority, while hoping to make money from their investment, realistically do not expect to do so. He himself did not set out to buy horses as a business, he explains, as his job at that time was creating golf courses. It is his opinion most owners are in it for the fun.

The Turf Club

Christopher has some early memories of the Racing Board when it was in Sunlight Chambers on Parliament Street in Dublin. He remembers visiting at a young age in order to cash in a winning Tote ticket and, as far as he recalls, at that stage the Turf Club also had offices in the building.

His next encounter with the Turf Club was in 1970 when he was invited to join, and he acknowledges that the Turf Club was not representative of Irish society at that time. Christopher, although he remembers being sounded out by the Senior Steward, never became a member of the Irish National Hunt Steeplechase Committee as he did not know much about National Hunt racing – Flat racing was his interest. At this time, the Turf Club had offices in Merrion Square, and he recalls that the various offices were spread over four floors and a mews building. Unfortunately the unwillingness of staff to travel up and down stairs meant that there was duplication of information between entries, declarations, accounts and other departments, and because of this situation, inefficiencies crept into the system.

By 1972, when Christopher, at a relatively young age, was elected to the position of Junior Steward by his peers in the Turf Club, there had been some modernisation. He says that it is important to realise that it was usual, at that time, that Junior Stewards would progress to the Senior Steward position, and the members when electing him assumed that he would be Senior Steward in 1974. In 1972, Joe McGrath junior was Senior Steward and he had introduced changes such as the publication of the photo-finish photograph, the movement of bumper racing from the position of being a Flat race under the jurisdiction of the Turf Club to that of a National Hunt race under the auspices of the Irish National Hunt Steeplechase Committee, and the changing of the composition of the stewards' group to Senior Steward, deputy Senior Steward and two Junior Stewards.

Christopher discusses the case of Denis McCarthy of Odearest Beds, who had been on the Racing Board. He explains that in the old days of the Turf Club, Denis would probably not have become a steward because the members would not have known him. However, once Denis had served his two-year term as Junior Steward, he was accepted, and he duly became Senior Steward. Christopher asserts that the Turf Club was somewhat archaic in 1970 and had not moved with the times, though since then, the membership has increased enormously.

Changes

The great changes that occurred in the 1970s when there were moves to increase the prize money for races and generally improve the industry, are recalled. Christopher is of the opinion that politicians did not like the Turf Club for three reasons, the first of which was that it was independent. The second reason was that government ministers who had responsibility for racing would have liked to have become members of the Turf Club; however, membership of the Club is for life and ministers do not always remain in charge of departments! He recalls visiting Taoiseach Liam Cosgrave of Fine Gael in the company of fellow steward Lord Killanin, and explaining that the Club was adamant that no serving politician could be a member. It is quite possible, he feels, that this situation may have caused some friction with politicians. Thirdly, he explains that historically, racecourses paid the Turf Club for the officials acting on a race day, such as the starter and the clerk of the course. A change had come about when racecourses wished to increase the entrance fee at the stiles. The Racing Board refused to sanction this but instead it covered the cost of the Turf Club officials on behalf of the racecourse. This system normally worked well, but a few racecourses did not transfer the officials' costs to the Turf Club, with the result that the Racing Board began to pay the Turf Club directly. This seemed to be the commonsense approach, but it caused a new problem when the Racing Board was now seen to be supporting the Turf Club rather than racing. This then led to the situation where the government was no longer willing to provide money for the Turf Club.

Christopher recalls that the major changes occurred during the tenure of Brigadier Sam Waller as Senior Steward. He thinks that some of these changes are for the better, while some are not.

Perceptions

After the demise of the Racing Board in 1994, the short-lived Irish Horse racing Authority took over, and its functions were taken on, in turn, by Horse Racing Ireland in 2001. These changes and innovations all occurred at a time when Christopher was no longer steward.

He does recall the widely-held perception that the Turf Club was a wealthy body. He explains that much of its funds at the time were only held on trust, and were not owned by the Turf Club.

International Stewards Conference. (clockwise from bottom) T. Blackwell, deputy Senior Steward of the Turf Club; James Holmpatrick, Keeper of the Match Book; Christopher Gaisford-St Lawrence, deputy Senior Steward; Denis McCarthy, Senior Steward; M. Guerlain (French Jockey Club).

As far as he remembers there was a figure of between £5,000,000 to £7,000,000 invested, which was money belonging to trainers, owners and entry fees. This money, as it was not owned by the Turf Club, could not be used to support racecourses as was suggested at the time. He feels that people did not understand the basic fact that the Turf Club had investments of less than a million. The figure which the Turf Club held on trust fluctuated, being dependent upon draw downs by the trainers and owners.

A controversial decision

Christopher recalls the controversial incident when Kings Lake, trained by Vincent O'Brien, won the 1981 Irish 2,000 Guineas at the Curragh, having beaten To-Agori-Mou by a short head. The local stewards, chaired by Victor McCalmont, disqualified Kings Lake as winner, and moved it to second place. Vincent O'Brien appealed the decision which was then re-heard by a committee of three appeal stewards of whom Christopher was chairman, the others being Lord Killanin and John Byrne. He thought that they would just support the local stewards. The head-on film looked awful, and their immediate reaction was that Kings Lake must be demoted, but the O'Brien party requested that they look at the film of the race side on. He recalls that the appeal stewards, before making their decision, then watched the film twenty times, each

" The Turf Club had investments of less than a million. "

time concentrating on different areas of the horse and jockey, and he says that watching the race sideways on there was no reason to think that anything untoward had happened. They came to the conclusion that Kings Lake's shoulder had got in front momentarily, and they came to a unanimous decision that they had no alternative but to reverse the decision made on the day by the local stewards on the grounds that they "couldn't find any difference in the horse's action at any stage in the sideways on film". The original result of the Irish 2,000 Guineas was to stand. The local stewards were fuming at this decision and Victor McCalmont offered his resignation to the Turf Club. Christopher remembers that the press, in particular the English press, were up in arms, but they were viewing the film showing the race head-on rather than sideways.

McCalmont's resignation was not accepted by the Turf Club, and after some time he withdrew it. Mrs McCalmont is remembered by Christopher as being very good during this time, as she would not allow the situation to upset their friendship. However, he explains that it did create an awkwardness for some time, because Major McCalmont was a longstanding member of the Turf Club who had given it great service.

Christopher Gaisford-St Lawrence was an active member of the Turf Club just prior to a period of extraordinary change in Irish racing, and he brings a most interesting perspective to the history of racing during the last half-century in Ireland. ■

Presentation by Harp Lager of a tankard in the Harp Lager Stakes at Baldoyle 1970. On left Sir Hugh Nugent (rep. Harp Lager), Christopher Gaisford-St Lawrence (2nd from left), and Johnny Roe (right), jockey on Place d'Étoile, winner.

Christopher Gaisford-St Lawrence.

Michael Dargan (left), Senior Steward; Christopher Gaisford-St Lawrence, deputy Senior Steward; Alan Lillingston, steward; Michael Osborne (far right), steward, at the Turf Club bicentenary dinner in 1990.

Sweet Farewell, owned by Christopher, winner of the Sun Chariot Stakes at Newmarket in 1974.

Paddy Woods on Arkle at Dreaper's yard in the 1960s.

CHAPTER 11

PADDY WOODS

> " At Gowran Park I went into the weighing room for something, and next thing, Tom Dreaper said "put on those colours, you're riding Arkle today "

PROFILE

Paddy Woods

Greenogue
Kilsallaghan
Co. Dublin

Born:
1930

Occupation:
Trainer and jockey

P addy Woods grew up near Fairyhouse racecourse in County Meath. He attended the local primary school, but felt disinclined to proceed with secondary education. He remembers frequently meeting Dick O'Connell from quite an early age, while the trainer was exercising his horses. Paddy enjoyed helping him, which gave him a keen interest in working with horses. Dick O'Connell held a training licence for Dan Moore, the champion jockey and later trainer of L'Escargot.

Paddy began to work for Dan Moore, whom he remembers as being a very pleasant man and a great trainer, but somewhat short of temper. Paddy rode out for Mr. Moore, and he recalls that in that yard at this time were a number of "pullers", which made Paddy able to hold a horse. He also cared for and dressed the horses but he did not get any rides. One fateful evening in 1956, a particularly acute bout of temper on Moore's part caused all the yard lads to make a decision to leave in order to teach him a lesson. Paddy recalls that some later returned, but he himself moved on to Tom Dreaper's yard, where his best friend, Charlie Reilly, also worked.

Tom Dreaper's reputation was already established at this time, and Paddy describes him as a genius with horses. He had a calm approach, never blustering or swearing. Dreaper's horses were doing interval training twice a week or so, which was innovative at the time. Tom Dreaper was also "a good living man", and the jockeys and lads were expected to attend church, as did their employer. Dreaper was known to be a good judge of a horse. In the sales ring he knew that others were observing him, and would bid for horses in which Tom had shown an interest. Paddy remembers that Dreaper's advice was not to buy success, but to buy a horse that you could picture going to a race. Paddy remarks that what Dreaper wanted more than anything was the truth, no matter what it was, and he utterly disliked being patronised.

At this time, in the late 1950s, Dreaper's owners included J. B. Rank, Mrs Baker and the Duchess of Westminster. The Duchess was the owner of the famous Arkle, which was trained by Dreaper. Paddy was privileged to ride out this wonderful horse almost daily for about three and a half years.

The jockeys at Dreaper's yard at that time included Pat Taaffe and Liam MacLoughlin, both of whom rode Arkle, and others were T. P. Burns and Mark Hely-Hutchinson. Taaffe then became Arkle's regular jockey, winning on 24 occasions. Paddy recalls that Dreaper's policy before a race was never to give instructions to the jockey; he knew the horse, and he also knew that the jockey was always trying for a win. In an illustrative anecdote, Paddy describes how jockey Peter MacLoughlin, who rode for Major Thompson, was waiting on one occasion for his instructions from Dreaper before a race. Instead, Dreaper asked Peter what he was planning to do!

The glory days of Arkle

Paddy rode Arkle out each morning, and he marvelled at the horse's intelligence and outstanding ability. He felt that he and Arkle had a good understanding, and he was disappointed when Liam MacLoughlin was chosen to ride him and Arkle won. However, Paddy got his opportunity one day at Gowran Park, when Pat Taaffe was due to ride Arkle but was found to be too heavy, and Arkle with Paddy aboard won the H. E. President's Handicap Hurdle in what was Arkle's last hurdle race.

The horse's winning form continued with the Punchestown Gold Cup chase in 1963 and the Powers Gold Cup chase at Fairyhouse in the same year. Then, in 1964, Arkle won the Irish Grand National at Fairyhouse with Pat Taaffe on board, and his first Cheltenham Gold Cup, beating the favourite, Mill House. In addition, this wonder horse won other races during this period, including the Gallagher Gold Cup at Sandown Park in November 1965, which he won by twenty-four lengths, a course record which remains unbeaten. Paddy recalls that he and Pat Taaffe walked the Sandown course before this race, and during the race, Arkle dropped back and went wide, but this was because Taaffe had previously seen rough ground which they were able to avoid and thus beat their great rival, Mill House. Paddy recently saw a restored film of the race, owned by Nick O'Toole, who, in 2011, commissioned veteran commentator Peter O'Sullevan to add the commentary. He watched the film at a hotel in Monaghan and was amazed at the huge emotion the win evokes among people, even today.

The great Arkle continued to triumph. He won the Cheltenham Gold Cup twice more – in 1965, by twenty lengths, and in 1966, by thirty lengths. Paddy remembers that the media travelled from England to photograph and film the horse, but this cut little ice with Tom Dreaper! Arkle's prowess became legendary, and in a fundraising drive on behalf of a children's athletic club, Paddy received the Duchess's permission to parade him at Tolka Park at a charity football match between jockeys and the members of show bands. It was stipulated that Paddy himself was to be in charge of the horse for the occasion. He recalls that he hired a horsebox and brought Arkle to Drumcondra, where he was ridden around Tolka Park and many photographs were taken of the very enjoyable occasion.

Then disaster struck. Paddy was with Arkle at Kempton Park racecourse in Surrey for the King George VI Chase. Going around the course, the horse struck the guard rail with a hoof when jumping the open ditch, and fractured a pedal bone. Despite this, he finished the race, finishing second. Paddy remembers the horse ambulance and the x-rays. The radiographer, who was used to handling humans, was nervous that the horse would kick, but Paddy assured him that Arkle would not. He had to break the news to Mrs Dreaper and the Duchess of Westminster, who came to Kempton Park on the following day. Paddy well remembers the photographers and journalists who arrived the next morning, one of whom offered him £250 for a photograph, which he declined. Arkle remained at Kempton Park for about eight weeks, but Paddy returned home after a fortnight to his family. Then, the horse was moved to the Duchess of Westminster's home.

Paddy Woods on Arkle winning the President's Hurdle at Gowran Park.

Paddy now recounts a tale, which adds further poignancy to the Arkle saga. The Duchess requested a meeting with Paddy at her estate near London very early one morning. She asked that he ride Arkle in the way he had always done for his morning gallop, which Paddy did and, on returning, reported that the horse was brilliant and in every way as good as ever. He thought that the horse should be put back into training, though Arkle was retired at this stage. The Duchess asked him to say nothing to anyone about the gallop. They met again next morning when the Duchess asked Paddy to put a head collar on the horse and to trot him. He did so, and to their dismay, Arkle took a lame step which signalled the end of any possibility of training him again. Although Paddy had left Dreaper's yard at this time, and was trying to set up his own business, he was asked to accompany Arkle to the Horse of the Year Show at Wembley Stadium. He was proud to lead him around the arena while the band played Arkle's song: 'There'll Never Be Another You'.

Interestingly, Tom Dreaper never ran Arkle in the Aintree Grand National, as he thought the race was too much of a lottery. Dreaper's dream was the Gold Cup at Cheltenham, and he certainly lived that dream as he was the trainer of five Gold Cup winners.

> " Tom Dreaper was a genius. He was doing interval training, maybe twice a week. "

Becoming a trainer

Up to this point, Paddy's life had been riding horses over jumps or on the Flat, but at the age of 40 he decided to retire. He was now a married man with a family. He considers himself to have been very lucky, as he rode good horses and had his fair share of chances. He won the Irish Grand National twice, on Last Link in 1963 and on Splash in 1965. He also won two Troytown Chases at Navan and the Milltown Novice Chase on Fort Leney at Leopardstown in 1964. He was fortunate that he never broke his legs, although he did suffer dislocation of one shoulder five times and the other on four occasions, though he believes this to be a family weakness, as his two sons, Eddie and Francis, have sustained the same injuries.

Paddy made the decision that his next career was to be a trainer, and he consequently asked Tom Dreaper for his recommendation, which was a requirement of the Turf Club. However, to Paddy's consternation, Dreaper declined to provide it. In any case, Paddy forged ahead with his application and went to the Turf Club to complete some forms, to be told that Mr Dreaper had been in and had given his recommendation!

The horses Paddy subsequently trained were predominantly from Northern Irish owners, such as Jimmy Robinson. With one of his horses Paddy won eleven races, and with another, he won seven. He remembers Jimmy Robinson as a staunch supporter who went on to recruit more

Splash, with Paddy Woods on board, winning the Irish Grand National at Fairyhouse in April 1965.

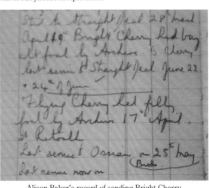
Alison Baker's record of sending Bright Cherry, dam of Arkle, to stud.

Paddy Woods.

Pat Taaffe and Paddy Woods missing the ball while playing football at Tom Dreaper's stud.

clients for his stable. John Harty, a local man, was riding for Paddy at this time, as was Eddie, Paddy's son. Eddie then moved to Fred Rimell in England, and Paddy's son Francis took his place. Paddy had runners in the Irish Grand National, and he trained the winner of the Kerry National in Listowel on one occasion.

Retirement from training

As an additional business venture, he began to sell an Irish horse feed from Waterford Co-Op. He knew many of the trainers in the area and the business became very successful. However, as he ruefully recalls, he was well-known in the area and began getting random calls for the foodstuff, which was not very satisfactory. Then Derry Casey of Waterford Co-Op contacted him, suggesting that Paddy should alert him if he decided to retire from training. The new business was prospering, and he explains that he did not find it difficult to make the decision to concentrate on it full time. One thing which helped the decision-making process was that the public road outside the yard had become very busy with heavy traffic, creating a concern for the safety of the horses. Today, Paddy promotes Gain Horse Feeds for Waterford Co-Op. He and his wife Phyllis have raised a large and successful family.

His son Eddie is prospering at his thoroughbred training centre in Ocala in Florida; he trains about 160 horses, some of which are sold back to Ireland. In an interesting example of family continuity, Paddy's son Francis rode for Arthur Moore, son of Dan Moore. Francis was an excellent jockey who won the 1995 Arkle Trophy Challenge and the 1996 Queen Mother Champion Chase, both on Klairon Davis. Sadly, a serious accident was to end his riding career. Francis married Niamh Cashman of Rathbarry Stud, and he now conducts nominations and sales for this business.

In Paddy's opinion, Arkle was the perfect horse; he behaved impeccably and got on well with everyone. He recounts a story which illustrates this perfection. In the normal course of events, Johnny Lumley in Dreaper's yard would look after the horse, but one evening he asked Paddy to check on him last thing at night. Paddy went to check him and was feeling along the legs, checking for heat or sweating, when he felt the horse jerk – Arkle had woken up. Any other horse would have kicked out, Paddy explains, but Arkle would never do that. He reflects on the fact that it was only in hindsight that he came to understand the unique privilege he had been afforded to work with a horse of such unique and immense talent. ■

Paddy Woods parading Arkle in the main arena in the RDS Horse Show.

Trainer Mick O'Toole. *Photograph Pat Healy.*

CHAPTER 12

MICK O'TOOLE

Great horses make great trainers, that's the answer! **"**

Mick O'Toole

Maddenstown
Stud Farm
Kildare

Born:
1931

Occupation:
Trainer

Mick O'Toole, one of the great characters of Irish horse racing, grew up in Dublin and developed his love of greyhounds and horses from Willie and Paddy Byrne, his maternal uncles. From about seven years of age, he "went to the dogs" with his uncle Paddy who had trained a Derby winner in his time. Mick left school at 14, a not unusual occurence at the time, and began training both dogs and horses. He was the first to bring a greyhound to England where he won the English Oaks about fifty years ago. Mick has had about 1,000 greyhound winners over the years. After some years training both greyhounds and horses, he decided to concentrate solely on the training of horses.

Mick began his horse training career at the Phoenix Park which was open ground in those days. About twenty trainers were there at that time, including Michael Grassick's father and Sir Hugh Nugent. The life of a trainer was somewhat isolated, he remarks: "You did not want to meet the other trainers, but to keep them at arm's length!" In Mick's opinion, not much help is forthcoming from others in this business – you really have to help yourself.

Mick describes the process of training horses as being uncomplicated: the horses must be got out, trained, put back in their boxes, and the trainer must find the most appropriate race for each horse's capabilities. He recalls that his first owner was an Italian,

Mr Tolaini. Mick recommended a horse to him through a friend and bloodstock agent Jack Doyle, and Mick reckons that he probably talked Mr Tolaini into buying the horse!

Mick began in business with about six horses, and he remembers jockey Johnny Murtagh (no relation to the present jockey), who rode Lintola at Edinburgh to become Mick's first winner. As he placed more and more winners, the business began to prosper. In the 1970s, he needed a suitable venue for his expanding business. Maddenstown Farm on the Curragh was available, having been previously owned by leading trainer Senator Jim Parkinson. Mick purchased the property, but he says it took a few years to really get going. His reputation now began to build and he attributes this to being in the right place at the right time, procuring the right horses and sourcing buyers and owners. In his heyday, Mick had close to eighty to one hundred horses in the yard. He did not breed horses, explaining that he felt it best to stick to what he knew best.

He enjoyed a positive relationship with his staff, and he believes that the right staff is vital to a trainer's success and he needs all the help he can get! Working with horses is a vocation for the lads, and he believes that there is no magic or secret to a trainer's effectiveness: working with horses is a vocation.

"Life is a gamble", he attests. In the early days, finding money for the business was the constant pressure, and it was necessary to find ways of getting "a few quid together". Betting was more important to him at that time than it later became. To Mick's mind, there was no need to make up any other pressures as he had quite enough to be getting on with. Once he was successful, he got great support, he says. There is no bigger gamble than training horses because one could go out of business overnight should the horses contract a virus, which would be catastrophic. Trainers need to hold their nerve; it is a sport for punters but a business for the trainers. Though a trainer has more losses than wins, Mick did not let this upset him as his philosophy was to get on with the job and to keep working. In those days, very few horses were insured as the owners considered themselves lucky enough to have bought them, never mind spending money on insuring them!

Mick remembers that in the early days a lot of support came from English owners, until Vincent O'Brien and Paddy Prendergast found new people to become involved. In his opinion, these two men contributed hugely to the Irish horse racing industry.

The trainer's work

There is little point is placing a five furlong horse in a four mile distance race – the right horse has to be chosen for the distance. As to the rest of the field in a race, a handicap system is used. Mick believes that training is not complicated; a trainer either knows what he is doing or he does not. If poor horses are given to a good trainer, they will still not win a race. As he remarks, "Great horses make great trainers; that's the answer".

You get a horse, analyse him, train him to the best of your ability, pick out a race to build up his confidence and go from there. He emphasises the importance of building up a horse's confidence:

if it keeps losing it will not improve. As regards the everyday maintenance, Mick emphasises the priorities: a thoroughbred horse has to be kept warm with proper sheets and stabling, it needs proper food and there are no shortcuts. The daily schedule goes something like this: the head man feeds the horses at around 6 a.m.; the lads and jockeys ride out about an hour later, once the horse has digested his meal; during this time the boxes are cleaned out; on their return the horses are washed down and checked for injuries and in summer they are brought out for grass. It is the same routine more or less every day, the only difference being a rest day after a race when the horses may be brought out to the paddock.

Naturally, Mick was not successful every year – sometimes plans went awry. A trainer has to go to the races well prepared and believing his horse can win. However, this does not happen every time and many variables may influence the outcome. Winning and losing never played on Mick's mind, though he agrees that winning is much better than losing! He emphasises the importance of a positive attitude, and many years' experience breeds a philosophical outlook, he says. In his early days, horses or greyhounds literally could not be given away, whereas in this present recession there seems to be a shortage of horses. He remembers when there were thirty horses in some races; now it is reduced to half that number. Breeding horses costs money, as does training, and of the percentage of horses sold, only a small number will prove to be winners.

Every race meeting attended by a trainer is important and it is vital to win somewhere, Mick explains. What is most important is a win at the festivals which is very good for business. When a trainer wins a Group 1 race he is kept in the public eye, and if you are not winning you will be soon forgotten. A trainer is only as good as his last win.

Mick has been travelling to the races at Cheltenham for many years, indeed since before he even had a horse. He does not ascribe much importance to the notion of a traditional Irish/English rivalry associated with the festival. The reason, he says, that Irish trainers go to Cheltenham is to win races, pure and simple, and here Mick pays tribute to Edward Gillespie, manager at Cheltenham, for his great work over the years.

Mick O'Toole saddled eight winners at the Cheltenham Festival. Notable horses include Davy Lad, owned by Joe and Anne-Marie McGowan (with a share owned by Mick), winner of the Sun Alliance Novices' Hurdle at Cheltenham in 1975 with Dessie Hughes on board, and winner of the Cheltenham Gold Cup in 1977. His best Flat horse was Dickens Hill, majority stake owned by Jean-Pierre Binet (with a small share owned by Mick), who won the Irish 2,000 Guineas at the Curragh in 1979 before finishing second to Troy in both the 1979 English and Irish Derbys, and landing the Coral-Eclipse Stakes under Tony Murray. Another of Mick's winners was Chinrullah which took the Arkle Novice Chase at Leopardstown in 1979 and the Arkle Challenge Trophy at Cheltenham with Dessie Hughes on board, in the same year.

At one time, Mick flew the horses to Cheltenham together with a number of other trainers who would combine expenses to reduce the cost. The aim is always to ensure that the horses are as fresh as possible when they arrive. The cost of flights is prohibitive now, though modern horse boxes are much improved, with air conditioning and so on. For a trainer, the most important day is Gold Cup Day, a day on which his horses are taking on the best in Ireland and England.

Mick was thrilled to be one of three Irish trainers, along with Vincent O'Brien and Paddy Prendergast, who had winners in 1980 at Royal Ascot.

The Harvest Festival meeting at Listowel was special because there was big money in Kerry in those days, and the festival often coincided with the Monday after the All-Ireland Football Final which made the atmosphere quite celebratory. On one occasion, Mick had five winners in a row at Listowel over two days. A trainer is always hoping that his star is in the ascendant, he smiles.

He has been fortunate to have had some of the best jockeys in the business riding for him, people such as Lester Piggott, Pat Eddery and Dessie Hughes. He remarks on the dedication of jockeys and the imperative to maintain an optimal weight. Lester Piggott's normal weight would have been around 10 stone, but he rode at 8 stone 7 pounds all his life. Tony McCoy could be 14 stone for his size but he could ride at 10 stone at any time. Apprentice jockeys also worked in the

" You didn't want to meet the other trainers, but to keep them at arms length. "

yard. Mick O'Toole had a great understanding of jockeys, and he had four champion apprentices under his wing at the yard. Apprentices would come straight from school and would stay at the yard until they were 25 or 30 years of age. As Mick remarks, jockeys have to be disciplined and dedicated. Their careers can be extended if they mind themselves, and today the food and travel facilities are much improved.

Looking back

Mick reflects on the fact that in earlier days there were not so many horses in the yards, and perhaps only two or three race meetings were held in a week. Nowadays there may be six. With fewer races being run back in those days, a champion trainer might have trained about thirty or forty winners in his lifetime.

Ireland has been a wonderful country for breeding and racing horses, he says, and also for producing top trainers and jockeys. He recalls the members of the Turf Club as being decent and honourable people who loved what they were doing and did it voluntarily. Although the stewards might make incorrect decisions as well as correct ones, what mattered was that they tried to give everybody "a fair crack of the whip".

Mick's favourite racecourse is that where a trainer has a winner, but there is nothing sweeter than having a winner on a big stage such as at Ascot, Cheltenham or Punchestown. All the racecourses were good to him he says. Galway is probably the greatest success story of all, going from a one-day event to seven days – Mick recalls that when it became a two-day event, it was thought that it would not last. He remarks that John Molony has done a fantastic job at Galway, and that the management there is very approachable and helpful.

He remembers the sales at Goffs in the early days, when the business was based in Mount Street, at the sales paddocks at Ballsbridge, and later still in Kill, County Kildare. His technique for judging a horse was to look at the limbs, and to look for something that could be improved.

There has always been a small element of bad practice in every business, but in Mick's opinion, such practices are dying out. However, once money is involved, there will inevitably be suspicion, especially from those who have lost and who need to spread the blame.

Glamour and excitement continue to surround the sport of horse racing, but Mick points out that working as a trainer and surviving in the business is a full-time job. About ten years ago he made the decision to retire because he did not want to see his business gradually run down. He keeps no horses now and he says that he does not miss the business. He continues to attend races every week, and he has not missed the Cheltenham Festival since the glory days of Arkle. His children continue to work in the industry. His daughter Margaret has been fortunate to buy some top-class horses from around the world for many of the big players in the business, and his son Ciaran is a jockey agent who has been lucky to represent a number of champion jockeys through his agency. The love of horses is still in the O'Toole blood. ■

Declan Gillespie and Mick O'Toole after Boarding School had won at Leopardstown in March 1990. *Photograph Caroline Norris.*

Thomas Berney senior, saddler. Photo taken for the *Hands* television series.

CHAPTER 13

JIM BERNEY

" I'm sixty years in this business.
The design of the saddles has changed, and the manufacturing of
the tree – the frame the saddle is made on. **"**

Jim Berney's great-great-grandfather came to Kilcullen in 1880 to set up his saddlery business. Over many generations since that time, Berney Brothers' Saddlery has enjoyed continuity in the family, with Jim's father and grandfather being master saddlers. Around 1912, the business moved to a more central location in Kilcullen.

Jim, one of nine children, was educated as a boarder at Newbridge College from 1945. While there, he recalls playing prop on the rugby team, with Paddy Prendergast playing full-back and his brother Kevin in the scrum-half position. Having completed Leaving Certificate and Matriculation examinations, Jim then worked in the family business, learning his trade. In 1956, when he was 24 years of age, he felt the urge to see something of the world and left Ireland for Canada. For a time, he worked at a saddlery in Calgary, and shortly after his arrival, he met up with his old school friend who was to become a wonderful friend in adulthood, Paddy Prendergast. Jim later moved to Vancouver Island, where he worked in construction, during which time his mother wrote to say that his father needed him at home. While at home on holiday, he met Patricia Timmins and they later married. Jim's father, Thomas asked him not to leave again, saying that the business was to be left to Jim and his brother Tom, so Jim returned permanently to Ireland, which he describes as the "greatest country in the world".

Jim and Patricia reared a family of two boys and two girls. Sadly, Patricia passed away in 2012, at the age of 80.

Jim's father Thomas junior had a farm in addition to the saddlery, which Jim also farmed in his time. Being a member of a large family was not a hardship, he says, it was a joy. He remembers his parents with great affection and often recalls their advice. Reflecting on his father's stories of life in Ireland before independence, Jim considers that things have improved immensely.

The working day in the 1950s and 1960s was more leisurely, with time for other pursuits. On a typical afternoon in the workshop, Jim recalls that Thomas might close the shop to play handball with him in the alley close by, saying that the work would still be there when they got back to it. Thomas also loved cycling and would race on the cinder tracks in Newbridge, Kilkenny and Dublin. He also had a hunter, and his brother, Patrick, who had a horse called The Tank, was Master of the Kildare Hounds. Patrick made farm harnesses for use with a trap or the plough – a craft that, as Jim says, has almost died out now, with the demand nowadays being for the tack which Jim produces for racing, hunting and showjumping. As a child, he remembers his father discussing his saddlery work for the British Army, stationed at the Curragh. He was kept quite busy there because of the large number of horses used by the army at this time. Thomas retired at 83, though he sometimes worked a little after this; he died at the age of 90. To this day Jim still uses his craftsman father's tools in the workshop.

Jim believes that it was his grandfather Thomas' business acumen that built up Berney Brothers' Saddlery. For example, when the British Army left the Curragh, Thomas bought a lot of equipment there, some of which is still used in the workshop to this day. Thomas senior died in 1955, when he was 85 years old.

In a tradition of continuity rarely seen today, the next generation is now working in the business. Jim is proud of his son and nephew, who continue the old traditions and who will keep the business alive.

The product

Berney Brothers' saddles are famous throughout the world. Jim provides an example of the complexity of the saddler's craft by explaining how a saddle is made. The first step is to get the front of the saddle to fit the horse's withers. Next, the weight and size of the rider concerned must be taken into account; Jim's trained eye can measure, just by looking at someone. The third factor is how long or short a person rides, that is how high a person leaves their knees, which determines the "degree of forwardness" on the flap of the saddle. For instance, a jockey rides with his knees almost up to his face whereas a hunting man would ride longer. All of these important details must be noted in order that the saddle may be fashioned to fit perfectly.

Jim says that although much shoe leather is made in Ireland, bridle leather is made in England, as there is not enough business in Ireland for the tanneries to manufacture it. Since he began as a saddler and perhaps even before, Berneys has been able to buy bridle leather from Sedgwicks in England. Jim knows that the leather he receives from that company will be of high quality. Leather is sourced from different parts of the world for the various pieces of tack. For instance, buffalo hide from Sumatra in Java, tanned in England, is used to make stirrup leathers, because this leather will not break or crack.

The saddle is stuffed with wool and lined with leather or white serge. On the exercise saddles, white serge is used which is very soft and kind to the horse's skin; this is what most racing people use even though this lining does not last as long as the leather lining but it can be redone many times over. Formerly nickel was popular for the metalwork on the saddle, but stainless steel is now used as this is of better quality and is a stronger material.

Besides saddles, Berneys not only fashion the leather for stirrups, bridles, halters, reins, bits and harnesses but also other equipment used by riders and horses, such as boots. Recently Jim made three pairs of Yorkshire boots, ordered by the trainer John Oxx. These boots are made of very soft material so that there is no friction against a horse's fettle or joint. A pair of boots takes about two hours to make.

An apprentice saddler first learns how to stitch, as this is the most important skill. Most stitching is done by machine, and Jim has a one hundred-year old manual sewing machine that he

Peter Berney (left) and Tom Wallace in the workshop.

bought in 1956, having seen a similar one in Canada. Since then, nine more of these machines have been bought, with three in use at present, and six kept in reserve, as they are difficult to source nowadays.

The original tools are still being used in the workshop. Jim cuts leather on a table in his workshop that was built sixty years ago. His knife, which has to be very sharp to cut leather, has worn down over time from being 1" to 1/8" wide – Jim considers that it is now at its best. He still works with some of his father's and grandfather's tools. His father's awl, which Jim refers to as "daddy's awl", was his father's favourite and is now about 80 years old. Another piece of vital equipment is the anvil, one of the items Jim's grandfather Thomas senior bought at the Curragh Camp. Jim uses the anvil, stamped with the date 1910, to rivet the saddles. As Jim says the rust-free anvil is indispensable and has served them well down through the years.

He reflects on some changes which have occurred in the sixty years since he began work in the family firm. The design of the saddle has changed, particularly the manufacture of the tree, which is the frame that the saddle is made on, has improved. Modern trees are now made with tempered reinforced steel, which can only be broken if a horse rolls on it, bringing

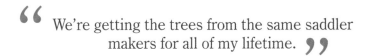

" We're getting the trees from the same saddler makers for all of my lifetime. "

the design, according to Jim, to perfection. With regard to weight, much of the materials used in a racing saddle are synthetic in order to make it lighter, and everything about it is thinner and narrower.

However, the skills required to make a saddle have not changed in his lifetime. As he says, all of the Berneys are masters of their craft.

A good business

In Jim's youth, it was his grandfather, Thomas senior, who ran the business, and who also exported to clients in England. One such client was a famous trainer, Atty Persse from Stockbridge, Hampshire. Jim's father Thomas at one time worked in England for Mr Persse. Thomas senior was in charge of the horse clothing section, which is still part of the business today. This includes the quarter sheets that are seen on the horses at the racecourses. Other items of horse clothing are blinkers, nightcaps, and rugs. Jim's late brother Peter took over the horse clothing side after their father's death. Now this is also Jim's responsibility. He makes the clothing, including binding the rugs, and his workshop is crowded with patterns of every conceivable type of horse-related clothing.

Jim notes that saddlery is a competitive business, and a number of the men who had worked for Berneys are now in business for themselves. However, there is continuity, too, in the current

Jim Berney in his workshop.

Jim Berney's father Thomas in the workshop in the 1930s.

Jim Berney happy at his work.

Tom Wallace and Jimmy Hogan, employees of Berneys.

employees and Jim mentions Benny Clifford, who has been with them 35 years; his grandfather had also been with Berneys, as had his uncle, Tommy Farrell. Another long-serving craftsman, who worked in Jim's grandfather's time, was Dubliner Joe Donoghue, whom Jim's father said was the best saddler he had ever met.

Quality counts. If a saddler makes a cheap product, then that will be his reputation. Jim maintains that a superior saddle made by Berneys could easily last thirty-five years. Jim gives as an example a quantity of thirty-year old saddles which John Oxx had recently left in to be repaired.

The customers

After sixty years working in Berneys, Jim says that he knows most of his customers, including almost every racing and hunting man and about ninety percent of the showjumping people. He has known generations of trainers and riders on the Curragh, such as the Welds and Prendergasts. Marguerite and Charlie Weld he mentions with affection and also others, such as Colonel Loder, Darby and Michael Rogers, and the Aga Khan.

Some customers have now been with Berneys for three generations, for example Margaret Zieg, whose father and uncle were customers and whose children are now customers of Berneys. Margaret's sidesaddle is in Berneys, a Mayhew model that is one hundred years' old, which Jim describes as an excellent saddle in very good condition which is now very valuable. The seat is pigskin with doeskin on top of the pommel and underneath. There is a safety spring bar that springs out to let the stirrup leather come out if necessary.

Hunting is a big part of the saddler's business, both at home and abroad. Berneys send saddles to Australia, America, New Zealand, Canada, France, Italy, and England. Their reputation for top quality leather and workmanship has been maintained through the years.

A landmark

Berneys is now a landmark in Kilcullen and there are few horsemen in Ireland of the older generation who would not know the famous saddlers. There are many photographs in the shop from customers, forming a significant archive of Irish equestrian history.

Jim has no plans to retire, and he recalls that his father would say that one should stop work only when one is no longer able. Neither he nor his brother Tom have suffered from deteriorating eyesight with the advancing years, and they still find the work interesting and very satisfying. He is aware that he has been fortunate, and he says he will be happy and ready when the Lord calls him. As for the younger generation, he is confident that the business is in good hands, and just as it was passed to him and his brother at a young age, so it will continue. His son Jamie has an honours degree in accountancy but he also works as a saddler. Jim is very pleased that Jamie and his cousin Thomas, get on very well together, and is happy that the Berney saddlery will be operating in Kilcullen for some time to come. ■

Jimmy Berney (left) with Peter Berney in the workshop prior to Jimmy's emigration to Canada.

Midge Carne, with jockey Francis Carroll, winner of the Newmarket Plate at Mallow in August 1947, being led by Rosaleen Tonson Rye. The horse was bought by her father as a foal for £10. *The Cork Examiner.*

CHAPTER 14

JOHN BURNS & ROSALEEN TONSON RYE

❝ I remember wearing the traditional
jockey's silk cap. **❞**

PROFILE

**John Burns &
Rosaleen Tonson
Rye**

Ryecourt
Crookstown
Co. Cork

Born:
**1929 and 1932
respectively**

Occupation:
Jockey and trainer

Both John Burns and Rosaleen Tonson Rye come from families with a long history of involvement with horses. John's grandfather trained horses in Scotland for Colonel Hall Walker, a member of the Scottish whisky distilling family, and one of the most successful breeders of his time. When racing was cancelled in Scotland and England at the outbreak of war in 1914, Mr Burns senior and his family brought all of the Colonel's horses to Tully Farm in County Kildare, to continue their training. The Colonel had purchased Tully (now the Irish National Stud) in 1900.

The family settled at Clonree House on the Curragh, with the horses stabled nearby at Ballymany. Following the Armistice in 1918, the horses returned to Scotland, but Tommy Burns, John's father who was born in Scotland in 1899, remained in Ireland having met his wife Stella O'Connor. John understands that his parents met at Roscommon races, and following their marriage in 1920, they lived in the Lumville area on the Curragh. They had four children, Jimmy, T. P., John and Stella.

Tommy Burns was a jockey until he was 52, having continued to ride after gaining his trainer's licence in 1938. His eldest son Jimmy was also a keen rider, and he served as a gunner in the Royal Air Force during the Second World War. He survived until the closing stages of the war, but in April 1945 he was shot down over Hamburg in Germany. John reflects on that tragedy, and on the sad day on which the family heard about his death.

The next Burns son, T. P., was a Flat jockey who rode his first winner at the Curragh in 1938, a day on which his elder brother Jimmy also rode a winner. John Burns was also a National Hunt jockey but with amateur status, riding in bumpers as his weight was not appropriate for him to turn professional. He worked with his father, training horses at Lumville, and he also enjoyed point to points, riding, as he says, over banks, drains, bushes or whatever was met along the way. He remembers that cross-country point to point races were held by every Hunt, such as the Meath, Ward Union, the Kildares and the Naas Harriers.

He recalls an event in the early 1950s when one of the Burns' horses, Upadee, unexpectedly won at Ascot. She had run races at the Curragh and in the Lincoln, but had no form as a four-year old. Although it was not suggested that anything untoward had occurred, the stewards wished to satisfy themselves regarding this unexpected win by questioning the owner and trainer about the horse. The trainer, Tommy Burns, was on board Upadee and Mr Galvin, who held the trainer's licence, was not present because he did not travel. The Irish stewards held an enquiry, removed the trainer's licence from Mr Galvin and told Tommy Burns that it was time that he retired as a jockey and to take out a trainer's licence himself. John recalls that Upadee was a very good mare, the dam of Vimadee, winner of the Irish St Leger in 1961. (He remarks that Vimadee was "a worrier", who did not train on after this win). Sometime after Upadee's win at Ascot, the Irish stewards gave Tommy the opportunity to retire, which he decided to do. As he now had no licence, the horses from the yard had to be dispersed, but as his son recalls, Tommy just soldered on and did not dwell on the matter. When he died, he bequeathed the stables to John and his sister, Stella, who still lives in Lumville.

John is reminded of other trainers on the Curragh from those earlier days: Jack Rogers and his son, Captain Darby Rogers, and grandson, Mickey Rogers, who trained Hard Ridden and Santa Claus, two Epsom Derby winners; and Aubrey and Cecil Brabazon and Bob Featherstonhaugh. He also recalls the Collinses, the Dawsons and the Parkinsons. He remembers the Curragh at this time as a busy place, where each trainer worked away on the gallops and everyone got on reasonably well, without the benefit of trainers' or jockeys' associations.

Rosaleen Tonson Rye's family also has a fine tradition with horses. Her father, John Tonson Rye, trained horses at Ryecourt in County Cork. She remembers him as being very keen on horse racing and completely self-taught. He had trained about one hundred winners by the time he retired, including horses owned by Noel Mahony from Blarney and Tom Egan from Cork. Rosaleen describes how John Tonson Rye got his grounding in racing from his cousins, the Delmeges in Limerick, with whom he used to stay. They rode and trained very successfully. John's mother was a relative of the Delmeges. The story is told about Rosaleen's mother Barbara, who was given £20 as a wedding present with which she bought a horse at auction named Flame of the Forest. It was trained by Jack Delmege, and when Major Scott rode it first time out, it was a winner. The Ryes had several of her progeny, including Dorothy Perkins which won quite a few races.

Both John and T. P. Burns rode several winners for Ryecourt, as did a local jockey, Peter Morgan. Rosaleen herself was a keen horsewoman. She used to ride in shows and had a very good show pony, Jack the Ripper, which won at the RDS in the pony class in 1944. This pony was by an Arab stallion out of a Welsh pony mare which her father had bought for £10 from a quarryman in Castlemore. Then in the 1950s she came third in the hunter class and later third once again in the small hunter class.

The jockey's life

The men of John Burns' immediate family were predominantly jockeys, and so it was natural that John should also ride. He recalls winning the second race that was ever run around Wexford racecourse in the 1950s, when he beat Pat Taaffe in the Maiden Hurdle on Easter Glory, trained by Dan Moore. In earlier times, a jockey's life was tougher, and it was difficult to get a ride on the better horses. As an amateur jockey he received no fee, but Flat jockeys might earn about £3 a ride and National Hunt jockeys about £5. His brother T. P., as a professional jockey, would face stiff competition for a ride. Naturally, the jockeys competed against each other for the better rides because only wins counted.

He recounts an amusing anecdote about a race which he rode at Clonmel with Alan Lillingston, also an amateur jockey. Three runners had been declared for a bumper, but on the day only two of those ran. John was riding a mare for Miss Preston which was poorly trained. Major Bert Scott was the race starter, and when the tapes flew up, John's inexperienced horse whipped around and Alan's filly jibbed, but did not move. John asked Major Scott to restart the race but he refused, so John gave the mare a kick in the ribs and she was off! Alan then came after him and eventually beat him to the finishing post. Major Scott, who was from the midlands and related by marriage to the Brabazons, had become a race starter after the war, and he is remembered by John as being very good, and also one of the great characters.

Unlike today, no health and safety precautionary measures such as crash helmets or back protectors were worn, nor did ambulances follow the races. John remembers wearing the traditional jockey's silk cap. His father Tommy rode for many years and did not suffer any major injuries. John himself was fortunate to escape with mild injuries and concussions, though his brother T. P. did have a number of serious falls in some hurdling races early in his career. Back in those days, a jockey did not face a mandatory break from riding; if he felt able to continue, he was allowed to do so.

Racing in the 1950s and 1960s

Racing was very different in those years, agree John and Rosaleen. There was little money to be made in the business, and bets were put on in order to make ends meet. Rosaleen recalls that her father was not a betting man, while John says that his father betted within reason, with firm awareness that there is no such thing as a certainty. With regard to the lure of gambling, John recounts a story he heard as a young man about the future King Edward VII of Great Britain who was stationed at the Curragh while Prince of Wales. Apparently, the Prince escaped through the window of a shop at the Curragh Camp and went off to the Curragh races. There he put £10,000 on to win but unfortunately he lost everything!

Race meetings were smaller than they are nowadays, and there might be only six races on the card. Each race meeting drew its own particular following. For instance, Dublin people went to Dublin meetings and rarely ventured to meetings down the country, and the country horses also stayed local. John says that just after the war, certain races were confined to horses trained in Munster, so that horses from the Dublin area could not compete against southern horses. The reasoning behind this was that the training ground provided by the Curragh produced better horses for Flat racing, and if they were to compete together, this would be disadvantageous to trainers from the south who favoured jumping and point to point racing over Flat racing. They did not enjoy an equal standard of facilities, and therefore did not produce horses which could race six or seven furlongs. Rosaleen remarks that at that time, the southern area races were held on alternate Thursdays at Limerick Junction, Cork, Clonmel and Tramore.

> " The trap from Ryecourt would meet them at Cork station, and the horse would be led behind the trap to Crookstown. "

Prize money has risen significantly since those days. In earlier times, no sponsorship was in place, and the racecourses made up the prize money from their own resources along with a grant from the Racing Board. Rosaleen recalls an occasion when her father's horse won at Killarney and brought home £300 in prize money. This was considered a huge win, and the Ryes felt as though they had won the Sweep!

A major change came about with Goffs' move from central Dublin. The auctioneers remembered by John Burns were Peter Nugent and Norman Colfer. He also recalls a time when English auctioneers were brought over to conduct the few important sales, as the Irish did not have the experience because there were few of these at the time. This changed with the arrival of American buyers and with the expansion of Goffs. After this, Tattersalls came from Newmarket and began to conduct sales at Ballsbridge and later at Fairyhouse.

John has some memories of the Turf Club from the time when it was based at the corner of Hume Street in Dublin, before it was relocated to Merrion Square. As he recalls, it was Major McCalmont who suggested that the Club should move to the Curragh, which did not meet with universal approval but which John considered a good move. As to Turf Club membership, in John's time it was comprised mostly of colonels, lords and army people who tended to maintain a certain distance. The Keeper of the Match Book seemed to hold an exalted position, while the stewards were also somewhat remote from the ordinary people, a situation which has now changed for the better, he feels. Stewarding has become quite strict, with cameras nowadays being trained on the race course. In John's time there were no cameras, but the stewards' secretaries would watch the races with race glasses. In the hurly-burly of a race, there was plenty of screaming and hauling within the bunch of jockeys – "the air was blue" as John puts it!

saleen (centre) being presented with the Tipperary Cup at Clonmel, where Midge Carne won by a short head from Teapot. *The Cork Examiner.*

Barbara Tonson Rye leading Dorothy Perkins, winner
the Garryowen Hurdle, Limerick, with jockey Jimmy Walshe,
in May 1948. *The Cork Examiner.*

Barbara Tonson Rye (left) with her daughter Rosaleen at Goffs sales in
1946. *The Irish Times.*

John Burns.

Rosaleen Tonson Rye.

There would be more banter in the bunch in National Hunt racing because the races were longer and run at a slower pace.

John does not remember much distinction between the various stables on the Curragh in his day, and horse training was a democratic business. A strong farmer who trained a horse had as good a chance as anyone else, he says. However, the business is very commercial now, and the thoroughbred is exercised in a strictly methodical and organised fashion.

He deeply regrets the fact that the Phoenix Park racecourse fell into decline and is now closed, and he recalls the party atmosphere which prevailed there during Horse Show Week, when a band would play and people were dressed up for the occasion. He remarks that horses were trained on the Park by the Welds and also by Sir Hugh Nugent, among others.

Transport

Interesting tales may be told about the transport of horses to and from races in earlier days in Ireland. At one time, CIÉ undertook all horse transport, with payment for carriage to the racecourse being paid by the Racing Board. Later, one was permitted to use one's own horsebox trailer, and expenses were paid per mile with the proviso that only one's own horses were transported in the box.

During the war years, horses were walked to the railway station, and John provides an example of what was involved in this procedure. Yearlings bought at Ballsbridge during Horse Show Week would be transported by train to the siding in the Curragh in the evening, and then led across the Curragh to their new yard. John says he has heard stories about people collecting horses at the siding in the Curragh and then getting totally lost in the fog on the walk across the Curragh on the way home!

Rosaleen also has memories of her father buying a horse at Ballsbridge, leading it to Heuston Station and both owner and horse travelling down on the night mail to Cork. The trap from Ryecourt would meet them at Cork Station, and the horse would be led behind it to its new home at Crookstown.

During the war, John Tonson Rye, Rosaleen's father, had quite a good horse named Bilberry which he once took to race at the Phoenix Park, where unluckily it was beaten by a head. The method of transporting the horse to Dublin followed the same procedure as described above in reverse: he first went to Cork by pony and trap, with Bilberry being led. Then he and the horse travelled up to Dublin on the night mail train, and on arrival walked to the Phoenix Park. John reflects that people were hardy in those days, and that horses were tougher and not so finely bred. Rosaleen agrees, pointing out that those horses ran on many more occasions during a year than horses do today. John remembers his father saying that he had seen horses being walked out to the races in Tramore from Waterford Station, and later walked back again. He recalls that the first man to drive horses to the Curragh racecourse in a horsebox was P. J. 'Darkie' Prendergast. This method of transport obviously saved the horse perhaps an hour's walk from a yard and ensured that it was fresher on arrival at the racecourse. In John's opinion, Paddy Prendergast really got flat racing going with his innovative ideas, and he provides as evidence of this opinion his memory of seeing Windy City – one of Prendergast's horses – running. He was the fastest horse he had ever seen in those days.

Both John Burns and Rosaleen Tonson Rye have had a lifetime of involvement with horses, and it is clearly evident they have witnessed momentous change in all aspects of the horse industry over that time. ∎

John Burns having won on Chotagora at Limerick Junction in the 1960s. *The Cork Examiner.*

William Robinson at an English racecourse.

CHAPTER 15

WILLIAM
ROBINSON

> **❝** I came along at the end of an
> era of tough horsemen and jockeys. They would ride anything,
> and the falls they took ... **❞**

William Robinson, one of five siblings, was born in Crinstown, County Kildare, and the family later moved to Phepotstown in County Meath. Horses played a great part in William's family history: his father, George, was a farmer and horse breeder who was known to be knowledgeable about horses and machinery, while his maternal grandfather, Edward Kennedy, bred the famous The Tetrarch. From early childhood, William dreamed of becoming a jockey, and as a professional, he rode and won some of horse racing's premier races. Those were different times. William remembers walking to race meetings at the Phoenix Park with the horse. After the race, the horse would sometimes stay there and go to Baldoyle the following week. Horses were brought to Leopardstown by train from Hazelhatch station and to Galway from Kilcock. His father always attended Galway races, and he and William would travel by train with the horses as roads at the time were poor. On arrival, they would walk from the station out to the racecourse at Ballybrit.

William remarks that life when he was growing up in the 1930s and 1940s was nothing like it is now. His memory is that he did nothing but ride and look after ponies and horses, and his ambition was to graduate to 'proper' horses. He admired Martin Molony, who used to ride horses for his father, because he was a very good rider, a true professional and a horseman. After boarding school which he did not enjoy because he felt cut off from his true life, William rode initially as an amateur jockey. He was restricted to riding only his own or his parents' horses as otherwise a professional jockey could be deprived of his livelihood. He was fortunate that his father had two of the best bumper horses in Ireland at the time – Windward Star and Silver Can.

Professional jockey

In 1956 when he was 22 years old, William decided to turn professional. There were risks involved, and a number of jockeys he knew at that time did not get the rides or the wins, and were unable to make a living from the profession. In William's opinion, this is less likely to happen today, as there is much more racing and thus more opportunity. He was fortunate that most of the owners his father worked with agreed to have him as jockey. As a professional, he won the October Handicap at the Curragh on Windward Star. He had already ridden for Mrs St John Nolan as an amateur, and he continued to do so when he became professional. He also rode for other owners.

William had to decide whether to ride as a Flat or National Hunt jockey; he chose the latter, a decision based on his weight. He reflects that, in earlier times, when it was extremely difficult to make a living, jockeys needed the fee so badly that they would ride on Flat, hurdles and over banks – if they got a spare ride at Punchestown or Fairyhouse they would take it. His own heyday began at the end of an era of tough jockeys who would ride anything, who took many falls and jumped fences far more difficult than those allowed today. He recounts an anecdote about Tim Brookshaw, a tough Yorkshire man, who was paralysed after suffering a severe fall at Aintree, and though he was not expected to walk again, he recovered, and he rode again too! William credits Lester Piggott with positively changing the manner in which jockeys were perceived.

William's first retainer as a professional was to Major John Corbett of Ballykinler, near Downpatrick, which lasted for about two years. He was next retained by trainer Dan Moore at Fairyhouse. In 1961, William won the Hennessy Gold Cup National Hunt Chase at Newbury, on Mandarin, for Fulke Walwyn, a leading English trainer, based at Saxon House, Lambourn in Berkshire. It was a dream fulfilled for William when Walwyn invited him to come to England. He terminated his retainer with Moore and accepted Walwyn's offer, staying there for nine years. There followed many successes. He won the Champion Hurdle at Cheltenham twice: in 1962, on Anzio, owned by Sir Thomas Ainsworth, and again in 1965, on Kirriemuir, owned by Dorothy Beddington. Both horses were trained by Walwyn. In 1963, William again won the Hennessy Gold Cup, on Mill House, trained by Walwyn, and it was here that he first met Pat Taaffe on Arkle in competition. Arkle had the misfortune to slip in that race. In the same year, William rode Mill House to win the King George VI Chase at Kempton Park, and he also won the Cheltenham Gold Cup on the same horse in that year. He well remembers Cheltenham Gold Cup day in 1964. Arkle had now matured and he won by five lengths, with Pat Taaffe on board, beating the favourite Mill House, ridden by William. He says that Mill House was a perfect horse – he could gallop, jump and carry weight, and if Arkle had not come along, Mill House would have been "king of the castle". Arkle, on the other hand, was an athlete and in a different league to other horses. In 1964, William rode the winning Team Spirit in the Aintree Grand National. Sometime later, he suffered a broken leg, and missed riding Mill House to a win in the 1967 Whitbread Gold Cup at Sandown Park.

Fred Winter was a jockey whom William feared meeting in a race because he was so balanced and strong. He remembers Josh Gifford, Stan Miller, Terry Whittlecomb and David Mould; they were all excellent jockeys, each with his own style. William says that no matter how friendly a jockey may be with another, once the tapes go up, everybody's your enemy!

It is every jockey's ambition to win the Grand National. William rode in the race eight or nine times, and was successful in 1964 on Team Spirit. In comparison to Mill House, Team Spirit was a small horse that had been bought by Joni Moore who had hunted him as a young horse. William had ridden him several times at Moores before the horse was sent to Walwyn. He finished fourth in the Grand National in 1963 and won the following year.

William explains that prior to a race he would walk a course like Aintree with Pat Hogan, one of the best horsemen, who would show him how to jump each fence. In those days, there was no apron in front of the fences, which was why so many horses fell. He credits Pat Taaffe as being partly responsible for the later introduction of aprons, which ensure that the horses do not begin a jump too late in front of a fence.

There were many Irish jockeys in England during William's time there, and he recalls that Jimmy Fitzgerald, a Yorkshire trainer, would remark that there was very little difference between the weigh room on an Irish racecourse and that at Market Rasen, with so many Irish jockeys in both places!

Mill House (second from left) with Willie Robinson going over the cross fence at Cheltenham. *Photograph The Sport & General Press Agency.*

William considers himself fortunate to have worked for former jockey Fulke Walwyn. He kept a firm hand on his jockeys and they were required to follow his instructions. He would stand for no nonsense. If another jockey had interfered with his, Walwyn would question his man and he'd have to defend himself, because Walwyn would make it difficult for the other jockey, who would have to be dealt with on another day! William also rode for Peter Cassilis and occasionally for Fred Rimell, which Walwyn did not like. When you are retained, he explains, owners are not impressed if you suffer a fall on someone else's horse.

Returning to Ireland

In 1964, William married Susan Hall, daughter of Major Cyril Hall who had managed the Irish National Stud. William retired in 1970 and returned to Ireland. Reflecting on his career as a jockey, he says you must be a little mad to go over those huge fences, but youth has a different outlook. To a young man, it is a challenge, as is hunting – as long the horse goes, the man will go. William maintains that he was fortunate not to have sustained serious injury in his career, although he broke a leg, a shoulder and the collarbones. He also suffered concussion, and there were times when falls prevented him from riding for a period. He is sure there were occasions when he was not fit to ride, but he took no heed. This is a jockey's way of life, he says, and there is the hunger to continue and to get paid! Now things are different, and a jockey has to get clearance from a doctor before riding.

> " If Arkle hadn't come along, Mill House would have been king of the castle. ""

After retirement, William began training in Ireland. Jim Browne was his first owner, who also had horses with Weld. He also trained some winners for Countess Fitzwilliam. In 1971, one of his winners was King's Company ridden by Freddie Head in the Irish 2,000 Guineas. He emphasises the fact that in order to remain successful, a trainer needs to win a good group race every year, such as at Ascot or the Curragh.

William also started to breed from a bloodline originating in Sunny Star, a mare owned by his mother and trained by his father. His sister also bred horses from this line. However, he regrets the fact that he had insufficient funds to buy what he himself wanted.

About twenty years ago, William moved to a property just outside Kilcock. Shortly thereafter, his business days came to a natural conclusion when, over a relatively short period, his mainly elderly owners died and he made the decision to retire. In 2012 he sold the property.

Looking back over the years, William reflects that he loved his life with racehorses. He went all out to win, and he enjoyed the fun of the ride! ■

Kilballyown ridden by G. W. Robinson in the 1957 Grand National. *Photograph Independent Newspapers.*

Team Spirit, with Willie Robinson on board, at Bechers Brook in the 1964 Grand National.

Racing at Sandown in the 1965 Gainsborough Steeplechase. Winner by one and a half lengths Mill House (left), owned by W. H. Gollings, ridden by Willie Robinson, taking the last fence alongside Ferry Boat, with jockey W. McLernan.

William Robinson.

Luke Lillingston (left), Alan's father, on Limrod (2nd), and W. J. Lysley on Patch (winner), The Hunt Cup.

CHAPTER 16

ALAN LILLINGSTON

❝ He smiles as he tells a story of his father, while riding at Derby, apparently asked the jockey alongside whether they needed to go around again! ❞

L uke Lillingston, the father of Alan Lillingston, came to Ireland from Leicestershire. He was always a keen hunting man who often travelled to Ireland to hunt. With his wife Susan, he was looking for a stud farm to buy here. When they heard that Mount Coote, near Kilmallock, in County Limerick was for sale in 1940 in two lots, they jumped at the chance. Major Watt and his wife Peg bought the other part of the property. Apparently, on one occasion, the Major was asked why he did not purchase the part of the property which included the avenue, and he replied that its upkeep would have been expensive and time-consuming, as indeed it was, especially in those days before tarmacadam became available. Mount Coote had previously been owned by the Greenall family.

Luke Lillingston volunteered during World War Two, and he served with the Leicester Yeomanry. He was billeted in England and his son, Alan, did not see him often as his short leave periods did not allow him time to travel to Ireland to visit his family. Tragically, in 1944 Captain Lillingston was killed in action in Normandy.

Alan recalls that his father was a very keen amateur jockey, whose colours were white, black and grey stripes. He smiles as he tells a story of his father, while riding at Derby, apparently asked the jockey alongside whether they needed to go around again!

Alan is the only child of his parents. His mother had previously been married to Charles Stanhope (10th Earl Harrington), the father of Bill Harrington. Alan remembers Bill as being a wonderful half-brother, almost a father figure, although never intrusive. Bill, who inherited the title at a young age following the death of his father in a riding accident, had lived at Elvaston Castle in Derbyshire. Following the sale of Elvaston, he relocated to County Limerick, and Alan remembers the wonderful furniture and paintings which Bill had kept that were part of the family collection. Another important male figure in Alan's young life was his uncle by marriage, Geoffrey Brooke, whom he really respected. Geoffrey, Alan explains, had a philosophical view of life, appearing very relaxed while not missing a trick. Alan lived with him for a time while he was racing in England.

Alan was educated initially in Kilmallock, and was sent to Castle Park at the age of 8, where Denis Pringle was headmaster. He remembers being sent to school two days late as a new boy, and he was wearing long trousers. This was unfortunate on two counts – he was late and every other boy wore short trousers! Later, he attended school in Yorkshire, and he recalls travelling alone to England by train from Kilmallock to Dún Laoghaire, and onwards by boat and train to Darlington, in Yorkshire. He later went to Eton where, as he recalls, he got his own room and had to look after himself. Later still, he "scraped" into university at Cambridge where he studied Agriculture, which he describes as having been a golden opportunity for him. He suspects that his half-brother paid the fees.

At home, his mother was looking after the farm and starting out as a breeder. Although Mount Coote was in a dairying area, during the war compulsory tillage was introduced, so the farmers sowed whatever crops were required. Alan remembers that during the Greenall ownership of the farm, about a quarter of the land was laid out in lawns, flowerbeds and walled gardens. Though his mother maintained these within reason, ultimately it became unsustainable, though they managed to avoid felling the trees.

Meanwhile, Mrs Lillingston was building up a reputation as a breeder. She married a man named Stephen Johnson, whom her son describes as charming. She died in 1952, and her husband remained in Mount Coote for a further three years, after which the property was turned over to Alan.

He was invited on one occasion to a house party given by Elizabeth Burke during the Dublin Horse Show, and there he met her niece Vivienne, with whom, on first sight, he was "totally struck". However, it was only when he asked her to marry him for the third time that she agreed, he says with a smile. Vivienne is a daughter of John Nevill, 5th Marquess of Abergavenny, who was very involved in racing and stewarding. He had been the Queen Mother's racing manager at one time. He had also been manager at Cheltenham, and later was Queen Elizabeth II's representative at Ascot until his retirement.

Today at Mount Coote, two further generations follow on, and since Alan's retirement a few years ago, his son Luke runs the stud.

The stud farm

Alan acknowledges that it is not easy to make a living from horse breeding. He remembers the first animal that his mother bought at Goffs in Ballsbridge, which went on to win the Maiden Plate in Punchestown, marking a successful beginning for Mount Coote stud.

"A marvellous man" named Jimmy Garvey worked with Alan for many years, having started at the stud farm when he was 15 years old, and leaving only when he retired. As Alan remarks, it is important to mark such loyalty and long service.

Alan's half-brother Bill had studs at Dooneen and Greenmount House, Patrickswell, and he would send young horses over to Alan in Cambridge for him to ride at point to points. When Alan was at university, he stayed during vacation with his uncle Geoffrey Brooke, who trained two year olds. This experience was excellent for Alan, as it gave him a fascination for training, which still remains today. However, horses were trained only in a small way at Mount Coote.

Jockeys and trainers

Alan recalls that it was Pat Hogan, a very strong, rather rough-and-ready jockey/ trainer/ huntsman, who started him on his riding career in what Alan calls the "P. P. Hogan School of Equitation"! When Alan was 13 years old, he rode his first winner in a bumper at Tralee, at 14 he rode his second winner over hurdles, and at 16 he rode a winner at a big meeting at Punchestown. A jockey would not get a licence today until he had reached 16 years of age, he explains. Considering his height of over six feet, he was a very good jockey and he describes himself as "mad to do it". He recalls making ten stone four pounds weight in the Scottish National, a good weight for his height.

Tom Dreaper was one of a number of trainers for whom he rode, and Alan describes him as being very amusing in his own fashion, and very straightforward to deal with. Tom Dreaper is renowned as the trainer of Arkle and Flyingbolt. Alan rode Flyingbolt at Navan at a pre-Christmas meeting, and it seemed to him that the whole yard was there. He did not meet Tom in the saddling arena, which was very unusual. The race set off and when Alan came to a dip with the horse cantering away, nothing was happening, so he applied the whip and as he puts it "the machine took off". However, having been first past the winning post, there was no sign of Tom Dreaper, but when Alan was walking past the trainers' bar, he heard Tom calling out to him "Did you come a bit too soon?" – the horse had won by nine lengths in the mud!

One of the crowning moments of Alan's career as a jockey was winning the 1963 Champion Hurdle at Cheltenham on Winning Fair. He was now recognised as a very good jockey, though he was only three years at the top, riding horses for people such as George Spencer and Tom Dreaper. His form gave him access to the best horses with the top trainers.

Then, great misfortune came his way when he broke his neck in a fall at Tramore. With no warning, the horse broke its leg and Alan fell badly. He remembers having a bad pain in his neck and asking to see a doctor, who told him to go away home. Vivienne drove him home, and though it was late as it had been an evening meeting, a doctor was called at about 11 p.m. This man gave him an injection and said that he would call around first thing in the morning. When he called, he made arrangements for Alan to be admitted to the Orthopaedic Hospital in Cork. Vivienne was delegated to drive, so, proceeding very carefully, she drove Alan to Cork. He clearly recalls the orthopaedic surgeon, St John O'Connell, who was well-connected with the horse world, saying "I'll fix him." He was to spend six weeks in hospital, strung up with weights, and a further six weeks in collars while he recuperated. He did ride one further winner, but his jockeying days were over.

Eventing

Though his career as a jockey had come to an end, Alan was able to continue riding. His next venture was three-day eventing. He knew Nat Galway-Greer, whom he describes as a very nice man, a wonderful man to pick horses and a master of the show ring. In addition, Nat knew how to play the market, and to show a horse with a view to selling.

After Alan's accident, Captain Harry Freeman-Jackson, a top three-day event rider, gave him Mercury to try out. As Alan remembers it, Harry said that if he got on well with the horse, he could take it to Burghley in the autumn. Nowadays, there are endless qualifications required to get as far as Burghley, the number two venue after Badminton.

> " It was only when I asked Vivienne to marry me for the third time that she agreed. "

Alan did well at Burghley, being placed in the top ten, which was quite something for a first attempt. He also began to learn dressage. His success continued and, with his horse Biddlecombe he was selected for the Mexico Olympic Games team in 1968. Naturally, this created great excitement. The team went out to Mexico and trained for eight weeks, beginning each morning at 3 a.m. However, in what was a great disappointment, just before the games began the horse damaged itself and could not compete.

Alan continued with eventing, buying young horses and showing them for a year. He won five winning medals and had one Supreme Hunter Champion – Josh – at the RDS. This was a very good period for Irish show and event horses, who enjoyed a niche of their own. He points out that an event horse has to be very good in three different phases in the competition: dressage, cross-country and jumping. Alan recalls that at that time, the emphasis was on speed and courage. Dressage has improved immensely in England and on the continent but not so much in Ireland, he says. He recalls the Irish Olympic eventers Patrick Conolly-Carew and his sister Diana, who were really very good indeed.

Alan explains that eventing was very much an amateur sport with a large military contingent. As he says, there will always be the military element to it, but since his time, amateur participation

Charlie Swan (left), captain of the 1994 winning team, accepting the Irish Australian Jumping Riders Series trophy from Alan Lillingston (right). *The Irish Field. Photograph Caroline Norris.*

Alan Lillingston in his prime in a bumper (far right).

Alan Lillingston, with his wife Vivienne.

Alan Lillingston (left) enjoying a day out with Luca Cumani. *The Irish Field. Photograph Peter Mooney.*

has increased enormously. He notes that there are plenty of yards now in England with a choice of ten or more horses for three-day eventers. The top riders have a great number of horses to choose from, for example the English eventer William Fox-Pitt has thirty horses. Eventing is now very competitive and the standard is very high. The sport has changed enormously since the 1970s. Alan nominates his best horse as Seven Up, which he bought as a three-year old from Nicholas O'Connor in the south-east of Ireland.

He says that he could not adapt at all to show jumping, but he did a lot of hunting and point to points in his youth. He advises that anyone who wants to go eventing should try hunting with the Limerick Hunt, to which in the early days he rode with his half-brother Bill.

Stewarding

Alan Lillingston has also been involved with stewarding, having been invited to become a member of the Turf Club (and Irish National Hunt Steeplechase Committee), which is responsible for the integrity of racing in Ireland. He has been a Senior National Hunt Steward, which is a significant responsibility, but he acknowledges the great people involved. One of his duties was to ensure that the programme of race meetings did not clash, and that there were enough horses in each high division to make each division worthwhile. He recalls his involvement in attracting a major sponsor for a chase at Down Royal, and there have been other big sponsors since that time.

In racing, the safety of the fences and hurdles is of vital importance. Alan stresses that the work of the Turf Club is undertaken on trust and ability. If a member made a nonsense of stewarding, he would not do it again – people have responsibility. He reminds us that the stewards work on a voluntary basis, sometimes driving across the country at their own expense. He himself has mainly stewarded in the Limerick area and at Punchestown.

Brigadier Sam Waller is called to mind, and Alan remarks that Sam was a little older than he, and was also a member of the Turf Club. He is described as a delightful and charming man, whose paperwork was always "immaculate". Others are also kindly remembered, people such as David Pim and Simon Walford.

All in all, Alan Lillingston looks back on his life at Mount Coote with great pleasure and appreciation. ■

Lady Helena Fitzwilliam (left) and Lady Harrington, mother of Alan Lillingston, at Epsom with a friend.

Cahir O'Sullivan, Keeper of the Match Book. *Irish Field.*

CHAPTER 17

CAHIR O'SULLIVAN

" I was responsible for organising meetings of the Turf Club, and for implementing decisions arising from those meetings. **"**

C ahir Edward O'Sullivan grew up in Louth village near Dundalk. He has had a varied career working in the financial area of business. He left Dundalk in the late 1950s to work in the General Electric Company in Dublin, during which time he studied at night at UCD for a Commerce degree. In 1959 he went to London where he qualified as a Chartered Secretary. Initially, he worked for a theatrical agency before learning of a vacancy in the Anglo-Irish Bloodstock Agency, where he subsequently worked as a book-keeper, a job which tied in with his interest in horses, acquired from his father, a Garda sergeant. After marrying in 1960 and following the arrival of two children, the O'Sullivan family moved to Somerset where Cahir had secured employment with Clarks Shoes, and following further years of study, he qualified as a Cost and Management Accountant.

Change of direction

In 1966, the family returned to Ireland and Cahir worked in Shannon initially, and later as secretary for a company in Newcastlewest. He became managing director of Myson Ireland, until in 1975 an advertisement appeared for Chief Executive of the Turf Club, which very much suited his skills and interests. He joined the Turf Club in February 1976, where he remained until his retirement in October 1999. He recalls being interviewed by Major Victor McCalmont of Kilkenny, Denis McCarthy, a bedding manufacturer from Dublin,

Billy McKeever, a baker in Ardee, County Louth, and Christopher Gaisford-St Lawrence, the hotelier and golfcourse owner in Dublin. Cahir's predecessor had been Lord James Holmpatrick. The new appointment had been made by the Turf Club in 1976 with a view to modernisation, at a time when it was felt that someone with a business background and up-to-date methods was required to take on the role of Chief Executive.

The Turf Club in Ireland

The Turf Club was founded in 1790 and it celebrated its bicentenary in 1990 during Cahir O'Sullivan's tenure. The Turf Club and the Irish National Hunt Steeplechase Committee are the regulatory body for horse racing in Ireland, he explains. They represent Irish horse racing on all matters relating to the rules and the integrity of racing. The Turf Club is also responsible for the administration of several charitable funds for the benefit of present and former participants in racing. The Curragh racecourse and grounds, administered by committee, are also owned by the Turf Club.

The rules regarding racing have changed over time, and during Cahir's tenure as Chief Executive, the Turf Club as a body met four times a year to discuss issues of importance. If the Turf Club members thought changes were necessary, these were made at subsequent meetings of members. Since its foundation, the thrust of the rules remains the same, that is, to ensure that horse racing is conducted in a straightforward and honest manner. The Governing Bodies were made up of the membership of around seventy of the Turf Club, and the fifty to sixty members of the National Hunt Committee.

Cahir reflects on the perception that the Turf Club was made up of many people with an Anglo-Irish background. Whilst this was true in part, he points out that all members, of whatever background, performed their duties voluntarily and still do so, except for those in the administrative offices which include the Chief Executive.

He is happy to pay tribute to the fact that in all the 24 years during which he worked for the Turf Club, he never encountered a situation in which a member took any action which was to the detriment of Irish racing. He does admit that the division of prize money did cause some dissent, in that the National Hunt personnel wanted a greater portion of it than was given to Flat racing. However, he explains that there are breeding implications which apply to Flat racing which do not apply to the National Hunt to the same extent. Most of the jump horses are geldings whereas the horses on the Flat are used for breeding. For instance, Sea The Stars was a very successful runner but is now at stud. The business of Flat racing is not just about the racing; it also involves breeding.

The Turf Club sets up inquiries to investigate matters when required. At no stage did Cahir come across a situation where any member did something which benefitted himself directly. In any organisation there will be cliques and lobbying, he says. He mentions Major Victor McCalmont, who was Senior Steward in his time, and describes him as a gentleman and a man of the highest integrity, who just loved racing. That is not to say that the Turf Club was perfect, and at times mistakes were made, as in all human endeavours. He reiterates that in his 24 years he never had to worry about politicking, or animosity between Flat and National Hunt, although there were personality clashes between members from time to time. In the end though, things always worked out.

In more recent times, party politicians have become connected with the Turf Club, but there is an unwritten rule that active politicians should not be members. When Michael Dargan was Senior Steward, he brought in former Taoisigh Liam Cosgrave and Charles Haughey at the same time, both as honorary members. The thinking was, says Cahir, that if Michael brought one in from Fianna Fáil, then he would bring in another from Fine Gael. He recalls Liam Cosgrave as being quite an active member, who attended meetings and acted as steward at Leopardstown. Honorary members, however, do not have votes.

Members of the Turf Club carry out duties on committees or act as stewards at race meetings. There is no remuneration or expenses available for travelling to race meetings around the country. As Cahir points out, this tradition continues to this day despite changes in the staging of race meetings.

Chief Executive of the Turf Club

It was never quite clear to Cahir what his remit as Chief Executive was, though he did ask the question at his initial interview. The Turf Club needed to be more efficient in the way in which it administered racing, and in the way that rules were implemented. It was felt that with his background and his interests, he was equal to the task. He says that after some months familiarising himself with the job, he implemented his own terms of reference, and made decisions that made things more efficient and commercial. He had to bring issues to his "lords and masters" who, at that time, were the four stewards of the Turf Club and the three National Hunt stewards. His primary boss was the Senior Steward. If a major change was proposed, for instance a change to the rules, then that issue would have to go before the membership of Turf Club or the National Hunt Committee, as appropriate.

When Cahir took up the position of Chief Executive and Keeper of the Match Book in February 1976, the Turf Club was based in Merrion Square in Dublin, and in the following November, the offices moved to the Curragh. His job was a varied one which encompassed many duties. His main responsibility was to ensure that from a financial viewpoint, the Turf Club was run in a responsible manner and within budget. This meant preparing budgets and accounts and reporting on the budgets. In addition, he had responsibility for organising meetings and implementing decisions arising from those meetings. He was responsible for obtaining legal advice where necessary, and ensuring that stewards and others were allocated appropriately to race meetings. Further duties of Cahir's included the computerisation of the office and the updating of race programmes and other information. He also liaised with the associations representing trainers, owners and jockeys, and with racing personnel in other jurisdictions. The Turf Club had some responsibility for RACE, the apprentice centre in Kildare, that the Turf Club took care of and also of the canteen which fed apprentices. A weekly journal, The Racing Calendar was published, so he proofread this for accuracy and to avoid potential legal issues. A good relationship with the media was very important, he says, and he communicated with media about race meetings. He ordered track inspections so that he could be in a position to communicate accurate information. Although he was employed to work five days a week, he explains that he was often on call, especially on race days.

Cahir acknowledges the team-work of others with whom he worked in the office over the years, such as his secretaries, including Mary O'Donovan, Sue Blackley and Ann Whelan, the financial controller, and the person who was appointed to deal with the Rules. Here he mentions Walter McDermott, who was later succeeded by George Walsh.

When Cahir O'Sullivan joined the Turf Club, Major Victor McCalmont was Senior Steward, with a deputy and two junior stewards. At that time, the Senior Steward was in office for three years and could be re-elected. Often the Senior Steward would be a man of some wealth. Major McCalmont lived at Mount Juliet and was a very wealthy man. As time went on, the Senior Stewards tended to come from a business background, such as Michael Dargan, who was Chief Executive of Aer Lingus, Denis McCarthy of Odearest, Pierce Molony, a businessman from Dublin, Lord Hemphill, John McStay and Roddy Ryan. At the present time, a Senior Steward serves for just two years and cannot be re-elected. He recalls Lord Killanin as being an

" "Michael Osborne was a legendary character. " "

interesting man to work for, a man with a high profile, most famous for his connection with the Olympic Games. He was interested in racing and had an association with Galway, but did not have expert knowledge. He also remembers Senior Steward, Michael Osborne whom he describes as a legendary character. Osborne had been managing director of the National Stud and, working with Sheikh Mohammed, was Chief Executive of the Emirates Racing Association, setting up international racing in Dubai.

Changes in the Rules

Cahir recalls one particular change to the Rules which was made during his tenure which concerned the introduction of a medical record book for all jockeys. It became mandatory that jockeys had to keep the book up-to-date, and bring it to race meetings so that he or she could be cleared on the day to ride.

Another change involved the introduction of portable starting stalls to Ireland. He recalls accompanying Lord Hemphill, Senior Steward at the time, to a conference in Australia. They travelled on to New Zealand, and while there, they saw portable starting stalls in operation. On their return, Cahir organised the manufacture of some similar stalls which could be moved around between various racecourses, and he gives great credit to Lord Hemphill for this innovation.

Cahir O'Sullivan, Chief Executive of the Turf Club, and his wife Greta, with H. E. President Patrick Hillery and Mary O'Donovan of the Turf Club, August 1976 at Áras an Uachtaráin.

Greta and Cahir O'Sullivan crossing O'Connell Bridge in 1958.

Cahir O'Sullivan.

The stalls previously used in some Irish racecourses were very cumbersome for transportation around Irish roads, while the new portable stalls could be transported by lorry. Over time, the portable stalls became outmoded, and today each racecourse has its own stalls.

Dope testing became much more sophisticated during his tenure, Cahir explains. The Turf Club introduced a rule whereby the winners of races throughout Ireland would be tested for prohibited substances, and it was part of his job to organise the testing laboratory. Of course, there were similar problems in other jurisdictions, and as Cahir points out, where there is a lot of money involved, gambles will be taken for gain. Although medication is allowed in the USA, in Europe there is an explicit rule that no drugs are permitted.

Another facet of Cahir's responsibility as Chief Executive was to help organise the Fixture List to be published in August each year. This was not always straightforward. Racecourses were in financial trouble in the 1980s, with some faring less well than others. Cahir explains that it is very expensive to run a venue for only five to six days a year. The Turf Club would endeavour to provide appropriate dates for each track so that financial rewards might be evenly distributed. However, with 28 racecourses in the country, it was not always possible to accommodate every one of them.

Some racecourses did close, for example Tralee, which Cahir maintains probably did not find it easy to compete with Listowel and Killarney. He remembers that Pat Crean was in charge of it in his time. Tralee Race Week became quite an important event, but as time went on the Rose of Tralee Festival itself eclipsed the race meeting. The closure of Tralee racecourse caused huge disappointment. However, Cahir explains, the impetus for the closure came from the racecourse itself, in that the fixtures were given up voluntarily. There was division among the directors of the racecourse company, with the majority in favour of selling the site for development. Cahir notes that this also happened elsewhere, for example at Baldoyle which was sold for development, and at Mullingar racecourse which also closed.

State of the industry in the 1970s

The industry was struggling to provide a service when Cahir O'Sullivan joined the Turf Club, but was having difficulty raising revenue. It is not a cheap exercise to provide staff for a race meeting, he explains. Officials had to be paid, though members of Turf Club were not. A team of people operates at the racecourse – the race starter, someone to judge the result of the race, someone to supervise weighing of jockeys and such matters. Many of the officials at that time were part-timers. The Turf Club did receive some state assistance for integrity services on racecourses through a grant from the Racing Board, which had the responsibility for betting. On the racecourse were the bookmakers, who were self-employed, and the Tote (or Totalisator), which was run by the Racing Board, a state body founded in the 1940s. Income at a race meeting was derived from admission, and the bookmakers paid a multiple of the admission fee. In addition, the Racing Board licensed bookmakers, so there was also an income from this. A portion of the prize money at a race meeting was provided by the Racing Board. With regard to off-course betting, the taxes raised there – at one point the rate was 20% – went straight to the exchequer.

However, with high value races being run in England and France, the owners and trainers were anxious that prize money in Ireland be increased. Obviously, owners wanted their horses to run in a jurisdiction wherein the prize money adequately reflected the costs of training. Commercial pressures entered the arena. Due to its longevity, the Turf Club was quite an influential body, highly respected both in Ireland and abroad. However, it was also seen as conservative. When the Racing Board was set up, provision was made that the Governing Bodies would have seats on the board, with the remaining members made up from possibly political appointees. Normally, the Chairman was a political appointee. As far as Cahir was concerned, at that time no party politics were evident, though there may have been some in-fighting and lobbying.

Things began to change as it became more and more difficult for the Turf Club to operate without adequate sources of income. Cahir gives due credit to Albert Reynolds, Minister for Finance, who, after extensive lobbying, decided that he would give an annual grant from the off-course betting tax to the Racing Board. The State was making significant profit from racing at that time. When Cahir joined the Turf Club, three to four days racing a week was the norm, but as time went on, this increased to six or seven or sometimes eight or nine events a week, depending on fixtures. Thus, prize money increased.

However, Cahir explains that even this was not sufficient for some. Big changes were coming in the management of race meetings. While Charlie McCreevy was Minister for Finance, he attended the annual Moyglare Dinner, and announced that his Department would give more money to racing provided the two bodies in racing, that is, the Turf Club and the Racing Board, would come together and streamline the administration of racing. Subsequently, in 1994, the Racing Board was disbanded and the Irish Horseracing Authority was set up in its stead. Later, in 2001, the IHA was replaced by Horse Racing Ireland Ltd. The creation of this new body was prompted by a march to the Turf Club demanding that it give up some of its powers to the state-sponsored body. When this occurred, Cahir had retired from the Turf Club. The change which came about meant that many functions which had previously been carried out by the Turf Club are now undertaken by Horse Racing Ireland, including advertising events, taking entries, taking declarations for the horses to run on the day, providing passports for horses, licensing trainers and jockeys, and so on. The State is now involved in the administration of racing.

All of this change came about because money was becoming scarcer, and races abroad had become more lucrative by comparison with those in Ireland. Sponsorship was good for about five or six races in Ireland which was important to keep up the status of the race, but overall, larger prize money was required. It would have created difficulties politically to provide State money to a private organisation such as the Turf Club, so a State body had to be created. It is now enshrined in legislation that the Turf Club continue in existence and be responsible for integrity in the sport.

The Curragh, home of the Turf Club
Since 1976, the Curragh Racecourse in County Kildare is the home of the Turf Club. The grounds are leased to the Club by the Department of Defence. The Curragh Racecourse is

owned by the Turf Club and is run by the Curragh Committee, made up of members of the Club and prominent people from the area. When a race meeting is held at the Curragh, the racecourse is responsible for providing labour on the day and all of the costs. The Turf Club pays for all the personnel responsible for integrity.

Cahir explains that attendance at race meetings is dramatically reduced nowadays compared to past times, and thus, income on the gate is down. Today, the main benefactors to racecourses would be television rights – the specialised racing channel, *At the Races*, shows all the Irish meetings on television. Cahir recalls presenting a paper on the development of television to the International Federation of Horseracing Authorities' annual October conference in Paris. At that stage, there was some indication that there might be a specialised racing channel similar to that in Hong Kong at the time. However, he admits that he did not have the vision to foresee that it would become available widely on TV as it is today.

His favourite – Royal Ascot

It has been Cahir's privilege as to attend race meetings all over the world, in places such as Australia, New Zealand, Hong Kong, the USA and Europe. He is adamant that the best meeting by far is that held at Royal Ascot. The racing at Ascot is superb, he says, and includes a wide selection of group races ranging over various distances, from the shortest at five furlongs to the Gold Cup, which is 2½ miles; also run there are the listed races and the handicaps. It is Cahir's idea of racing heaven to be at Ascot in the month of June!

Cahir O'Sullivan's legacy

Cahir feels a great loyalty to the Turf Club. He has seen it from the inside as an executive and following his retirement, he became a member and was later steward for two years. He feels that on his retirement he left behind an administrative structure which is efficient, and it is his hope is that he succeeded in streamlining the administration of the Turf Club and taking care of the staff.

His view of the future

During his tenure as Chief Executive from 1976 to 1999, Cahir has seen the administration of the race meetings change from being done mainly on a voluntary basis to being less so today. He explains that at every meeting there are five stewards: one is stipendiary (i.e. paid) and the other four are voluntary (i.e. Turf Club members or National Hunt members). In his view, this system is working well, as there is a constantly changing group of stewards who meet infrequently with trainers and other personnel involved in the industry; familiarity must not be allowed to breed contempt, he says. However, he feels that the voluntary element in the sport will not continue indefinitely due to financial and time pressures on the people today.

Cahir O'Sullivan finds it difficult to be optimistic about the future, as he feels that the future for Irish racing is bleak. He believes that the economic situation in Irish racing is quite precarious, and due to the heights reached over the past ten years, the lows can be bad indeed. He says that he wonders how trainers are existing at the moment, as they have to be paid by the owners, and due to the present recession payment is not always guaranteed. However, racing is a great survivor, he declares in a more optimistic vein. With regard to increasing income from betting, this is an area which has changed completely. Bets are no longer placed on a horse only to win. There is also online and offshore betting. The problem with offshore betting is that it is not involved with the development of the sport in Ireland. He is hopeful, however, that this will change as a result of strong lobbying behind the scenes.

All in all, Cahir O'Sullivan counts himself privileged to have worked in an area in which he was totally involved, and in which he has always had a consuming interest. He is now a widower, and he states that it is racing that keeps him engaged as he discusses races past with like-minded individuals, and looks forward with eagerness and fascination to the next race meeting. ■

Michael Osborne with Cahir O'Sullivan (right).

Fairy Bridge with Tommy Murphy on board at the Phoenix Park.

CHAPTER 18

TOMMY MURPHY

" He greatly enjoyed his apprenticeship though it was a seven days a week job, which included helping out with fences or riding on Sunday afternoons. **"**

Tommy Murphy

**Ballydoyle
Co. Tipperary**

Born:
1936

Occupation:
Jockey

Tommy Murphy comes from a fishing and farming family from Kilmore Quay in County Wexford, and he is one of seven children, He grew up with ponies and working horses on the family farm. He has had a highly successful career, initially as a jockey and later as headman at one of the most prestigious yards in Ireland. In earlier days, he explains, it was customary for most trainers to employ their own jockeys. In 1951, when he was fourteen, he left school and in his first time away from home, he began his jockey apprenticeship, working for five years with Milo Walsh in Waterford. Tommy remembers Milo as a decent employer who paid him ten shillings a week, at a time when the Curragh apprentices were earning two shillings and sixpence. He greatly enjoyed his apprenticeship though it was a seven days a week job, which included helping out with fences or riding on Sunday afternoons.

Walsh had about twelve horses, and Tommy's first win was on Fabrice at the Phoenix Park in a one mile race. This was an excellent start for him and it helped give him confidence. He reflects that the life of a jockey was tougher at that time – everything was rough, even the timber rails on the racetrack, which could cause serious injury to a jockey's legs. In the early days he would travel with the horses to the races and saddle them up himself.

England

When Tommy's apprenticeship was completed in 1956, he decided to take a gamble, and he moved to England where he had no trainer, but he thought he would try his luck. He had married Celia Crowdle from Kilmacthomas at the age of 21, and so he had new responsibilities. He worked initially at Epsom for about six months, and he then moved to the Duke of Norfolk's stables, where he worked for four years. He remembers very kindly the Duke and Duchess. Also there at the time was Arthur 'Scobie' Breasley, the Australian jockey. At this stage, Tommy was getting many good rides, and was enjoying life very much.

He then moved to Fred Rimell's stables, working for the National Hunt trainer. This was a very exciting move, but unfortunately, he was not getting the best rides although he had been assured that he would. After a year, he left to begin work in Somerset for a private trainer named Harding. He remembers that it was difficult to be an Irish jockey in England at this time, although he emphasises that he preferred to work for a headman who was English rather than Irish. Irish headmen, as he puts it, "loved to hear themselves shouting".

Returning home

In 1964, Tommy heard about a possible job as head lad at Clem Magnier's stable at Rathvale, County Meath, and having secured this post, he returned to Ireland with his wife and two children. He describes the following decade working with Clem as great years, each one better than the last. In 1972, he won the Gloucester Hurdle at Cheltenham, on Noble Life, owned by Matt Gallagher and trained by Christy Grassick. This win was hugely satisfying as he beat Comedy of Errors, trained by Fred Rimell, the trainer who had failed to give him good rides! His success continued with two winners in the Galway Hurdle and a win in the Carrolls Hurdle at Dundalk. He won again on Pianissimo at the Phoenix Park. This was a five furlong dash for two-year olds, which could be over in less than a minute.

Life was good for Tommy at this time; he was riding a lot more and riding more winners. However, he often felt concerned for apprentices who were not getting rides, and expressed this concern to trainers on a number of occasions. His concern centred on the ability of these men to make a living, though he believes that things have now improved. Those who work in horse racing with very little financial reward are the truly dedicated people, he believes.

A jockey's fee then was £5 for riding, with 10% of any winnings if the trainer paid it over. However, Tommy remembers cases where a jockey was not paid any winnings, and he believes it is best that it is now paid through the Turf Club. Tommy has some good memories of his colleagues who would share transport in order to reduce expenses. The top jockeys of the time included Tommy Carberry, his friend Pat Taaffe, Bobby Beasley and Bobby Coonan.

Tommy was delighted to be invited to attend Clem Magnier's 95th birthday party in 2012. He has great memories of his time with Clem, a man who gave him excellent opportunities in both hurdles and flat races. Tommy worked hard, never missing a day, but Clem was always very supportive, and that was sufficient for Tommy.

Ballydoyle

On one occasion, Tommy was told that Vincent O'Brien was looking for a jockey at his stables at Ballydoyle in County Tipperary. On arriving for interview, his first impression of the stables was that it was "unreal", as it was evident that only the best of everything was acceptable there. He secured the post, and there followed eight very good years. While Lester Piggott was the number one jockey, Vincent always ensured that Tommy got good rides which kept his interest and anticipation keen.

Some of his successes included winning the Irish 1,000 Guineas at the Curragh on Lady Capulet in 1977, beating stable mate Lester Piggott by three lengths. That same year, in the Irish St Leger at the Curragh, he beat Piggott again on the favourite Transworld, owned by Simon Fraser and trained by Vincent O'Brien, winning by four lengths.

Tommy remembers Vincent O'Brien as a straightforward man who was terrific to work for; he allowed a jockey in a race to use his discretion according to the manner in which events played out on the track. Vincent's policy was to discuss tactics the day before the race, with nothing being said in the parade ring on the day.

On retiring from riding after thirty years in 1980, Tommy considers himself lucky to have sustained only a fractured leg, punctured lungs, and a fractured collar bone! When he retired as a jockey, he went to work with Mick O'Toole for a year, and he remarks that Mick was a great character who had a completely different personality to that of Vincent O'Brien, but he was also very good to Tommy.

Some time after this, Tommy returned to work for Vincent O'Brien as an assistant, or headman, and he remained at Ballydoyle, looking after the horses for about twenty years. There was a huge sense of pride involved in working for Ballydoyle, the best yard in the country. There was a strict routine with each and every task completed correctly, as a horse has to be sound and feeling well for a race. As Tommy remarks, there is nothing glamorous about this work, and there is no margin at all for error. The yard was so well organised that everyone knew where they should be at any given time; 1 p.m. to 3 p.m. daily was the horses' rest time, when nobody was allowed into the yard and silence prevailed. He reflects that, in a way, a headman gets to know the horses almost better than his own family, and that they would know him too. Tommy always kept a close eye on the horses, checking them regularly throughout the day. He remarks that though repetitive, this work is never boring for anyone who loves working with horses.

As headman, Tommy got on very well with Vincent O'Brien, who was, he says, an excellent employer. Every afternoon, Vincent would go for a stroll on the gallops and Tommy would join him, and they would discuss the horses and anything else that came to mind. Tommy thinks that his employer was shy in a group, but had quite a good sense of humour which was particularly evident on a one to one basis.

A jockey's life

Much change has occurred in the horse racing world in Tommy's time. In his early days, there were no starting stalls, with tapes or string being used. There was little emphasis on safety: jockeys did not wear crash helmets, and the timber rails at the tracks were unsafe. On one occasion, he had a bad fall at Tramore and a few of the horses galloped over him. Many bad falls occurred at Tramore he explains; it is a Flat race so the horses are travelling at speed, and coming down the hill is the probable place for falls.

However, you just get back up again – it's like riding a bike he says. A jockey gets so used to the life it becomes second nature after a time. A jockey is only as good as his last race, and if you ride a poor race, you're back to square one again. On a few occasions in his career some of the other lads held him in and prevented him from making a break for the finishing post, a misdemeanour which nowadays would cause a jockey to be brought up before the stewards. Tommy himself was never called up in front of the Turf Club, neither was he suspended, although he was sometimes called a "dirty jockey". At every race, a jockey meets the same fellow competitors, and some of these might be friends or from the same stable. However, it is the jockey who must decide whether to take his chances, and to balance a ride between getting sandwiched in or running wide. This is easier on wide tracks but less so on tight tracks like Tramore, Kilbeggan or Galway. Indeed, Tommy recalls, from firsthand experience, that orders cannot be given to jockeys in Galway as so many unpredictable things may happen there on the day. A jockey has to be quick-wittted, and his key advice is "Never look back when riding"!

" Never look back when riding! "

On the subject of gambling, Tommy says he knows little about it as a jockey is not allowed to gamble and, in any case, he has no interest. He recalls riding horses that opened at 33/1 and then reduced to 13/2. It was cheaper to live in earlier days, and perhaps that meant that comparatively more money was spent on gambling.

Michael Moylan from Newbridge was Tommy's valet. He was excellent at his job, and Tommy remarks that Michael's father was a great jockey in his day. He explains that a valet must have everything prepared for the jockey, especially when weight is vital. His own saddle, which had to be both light and very strong, was tailor-made for him by Berneys of Kilcullen.

Tommy Murphy retired from riding in 1994, and continued to work at Ballydoyle until 2005. Occasionally he visits the yard where he meets with Aidan O'Brien to take a look at the horses and to discuss equine matters. Though he has lived a hard and competitive life, Tommy feels that he has been lucky. He is aware that some jockeys work their whole lives with never a winner, yet they still continue. Tommy's son Andrew now works in Ballydoyle, and thus the strong family link and the great love of horses survives to this day. ■

Noble Life, winner of the Gloucester at Cheltenham in 1972, photographed in the old enclosure.

Pat Keating and Tommy Murphy (left) in 2006.
The Irish Field. Photograph Healy.

Tommy Murphy.

Sonia Rogers.

CHAPTER 19

SONIA ROGERS

“ We thought of nothing but work, and that's
all we did all day and all night ... ”

S onia Rogers née Pilkington has lived a full and interesting life. By her own admission, she has always been very independent, possibly because she moved home a number of times as a child. Her love of art was fostered when, at 16 years of age during a visit to Florence, was tutored by a White Russian *emigrée*. She attended a smart finishing school in Paris and had a London season. She then set off to work her way around the globe. She washed cars in California, was a housemaid in Banff and learned to type at a secretarial school in Dublin.

Sonia's mother had remarried and come to live in Ireland with her husband, Tony Burke. They restored Stackallen which had a fine stable yard, accommodating many hounds and hunters. Sonia hunted with the Ballymacad, Meath and Ward Hunts, and remembers her mother as a great horsewoman who rode sidesaddle, and was a very good cross-country rider. After her step-father's death, Sonia helped her mother to run the stud which had about twenty mares at that time. She then spent two years as secretary at Cloghran Stud in County Dublin which was owned by Colonel John Samuelson, and she recalls Above Suspicion and Whistler, two famous horses there at that time. During holidays and when she was between jobs elsewhere, Sonia made frequent trips to Ireland and enjoyed hunting here. In 1965, she married Tim Rogers of Airlie Stud in Lucan, County Dublin.

Captain Tim Rogers had been *aide-de-camp* to Sir Winston Churchill during the Second World War, and the men remained good friends. Tim was also very friendly with Christopher Soames and his wife Mary who visited Ireland regularly. Tim had worked with his father Darby, who had trained many winners. After the war, Tim built up the business at Airlie Stud where his first horses were Vienna and High Hat which he had bought from Churchill.

Grangewilliam Stud

When Grangewilliam came on the market, Tim and Sonia could not afford to buy it outright, but with a loan from Sonia's mother, Sonia's own savings and Tim's borrowings, they bought the 268 acres for £90,000 in 1965. Sonia recalls that the previous owner of Grangewilliam was German. The story goes that he had suddenly vacated the property, leaving everything behind including his bedroom slippers! The property included many out-buildings and cottages, which was very useful for the business. Further purchases were made on a partnership basis; Simmonstown was bought in the same year in partnership with John Byrne and Ronald de Chambure.

As with any new endeavour, Sonia remembers that she and Tim worked exceedingly long hours. Everything was invested in the business, and they did not take a holiday for years.

Tim's particular area of expertise was stallions which he kept for two or three years and then sold on, although sometimes an exceptional stallion such as Habitat would not be sold. During the 1970s, there were 44 shares in this stallion at £10,000 each and he was covering mares at £80,000 a year. In those days, the buyers were often Japanese. Sonia has good memories of Alec Head and Ronald de Chambure who were excellent partners in business. It was customary at the time for breeding horses to be owned by syndicates, as the funds for an individual to buy one outright tended not to be available. The syndicates were complex to operate as there were perhaps forty shareholders and forty or so mares were covered. Sonia believes that Tim was probably the first to introduce foal shares. This might occur if the owner of a mare could not afford the fee for a prestigious stallion, so the stallion owner might produce the nomination and the two owners would each own half of the offspring.

In the 1970s, Tim was the first foreigner to be allowed to buy a stud farm in New Zealand. As Sonia remarks, New Zealand, Kentucky and Ireland are the three best places to grow horses. She maintains that it was Tim, with Charles Haughey, who proposed that shares in stallions should be tax-free as an incentive for Ireland. Many people credit Tim Rogers as the founder of the modern Irish bloodstock industry.

By the time of his death in January 1984, Tim had almost a monopoly on stallions, and was the premier source for advice on the subject. He and Robert Sangster were partners before Coolmore Stud was started; Sangster then went into partnership with Vincent O'Brien and John Magnier. Sonia remarks that John has always been a friend, and has been very helpful to her.

Taking over the stud

Throughout her married life, Sonia tended to focus her energies on the family, the well-being of the assistants who lived in accommodation on the property, and on providing hospitality for visitors. She had little to do with the bloodstock business other than travelling to the New Zealand stud for the January sales. However, when her husband died after a six-year illness, Sonia recalls enquiries about whether she would continue with the stud, and she says this made her realise that she did indeed want to continue. The stud at the time employed about 100 people, and there were about fourteen stallions and over 100 mares there. This was a difficult time for the business, and Sonia found that people had to be repeatedly requested to pay their debts. She can recall having to wait outside certain houses in order to get paid. Her brother-in-law, Mickey Rogers, was a good judge of a horse and was helpful to her at this difficult time, but sadly he passed away a short time later.

When Tim died, Anthony and John, their two sons were twelve and fourteen years old respectively. Six years later, Sonia asked them if they were interested in working at the stud, because if either was, she would continue with the business for his sake. Anthony, who had always been interested in animals, said that he would like the work. Sonia encouraged him to travel abroad for experience, and he spent about nine years working for trainers and various studs in Australia and California. Anthony is now manager of the stud.

In earlier days, Sonia had worked at her mother's stud and for Kazimierz Bobinsky at the BBA for about a year. Bobinsky wrote *Family Tables of Racehorses*, the definitive textbook on

Captain Tim Rogers at the sales.

thoroughbred family structure. However, she was conscious of not having the required training in stud work, and she had never spent time foaling. She therefore employed Julian Lloyd as an assistant at the stud. At this time, Coolmore Stud was gaining in prominence, and Sonia was aware that this was where the major finance would go. She took a conscious decision to sell the stallions and buy some good mares. Thus, following small beginnings and over a period of twenty-five years, the stud now has a very good group of mares. In the current recession, she is glad that she does not have stallions because she knows that she would again have to chase creditors.

Breeding is a risky business where a lot of money can be lost very quickly. Sonia advises that a stud needs to keep changing the mares and have a clear-out every year. Sentimentality cannot enter into it, and fortunately, by and large, she does not get attached to the animals as she knows that it is a commercial business.

The stud sells foals, yearlings and fillies out of training at the sales in Goffs, USA, England and sometimes France. Recently, Sonia sold a filly that had won by a record eighteen lengths in a one-mile maiden race at Dundalk. David Watchman took half, and this sale will pay the bills until the yearling sales come around again. With regard to sales, she explains that she decides beforehand on a reserve price. Sometimes she sells at a price that is lower than she would like,

" You've got to learn your trade, and watch yourself. "

and sometimes she is lucky to get a better price than she had hoped, but it all averages out in the end. With a filly, she can keep it and train it if it is any good; if it does not win a race, she can still breed from it. A colt is of no use to her because she is not interested in stallions. If a filly is kept for training, Sonia might lease to a partner because the training bill for two years might come to €25,000-€30,000. It is all a gamble, she says, adding that she is not a gambler on something that is out of her control. Betting on a horse at the races means also gambling on the trainer and jockey too. Her feeling is that she is gambling already in her business and that is quite enough!

Many of their staff have been with them for years, and there are now about thirty employees. Anthony is in charge of the whole operation. The general manager is David Sullivan, who had worked previously in a stud in Kentucky with Sonia's nephew, who recommended him. David's eldest child has also worked for Sonia, and is now in the USA.

The business of breeding

Sonia remembers when the Arabs began to come to Ireland. Colonel Dick Warden, a friend of her mother's, produced the first winner for Sheikh Mohammed bin Rashid Al Maktoum, which aroused much interest. She remembers Sheikh Mohammed coming to visit Tim on occasion, and she maintains that the Irish horse racing industry is fortunate to have access to the Arab

Tim and Sonia Rogers on their wedding day.

money. She says that the Sheikh did not buy at Tattersalls one year, but of necessity she sold all her yearlings, getting probably less than optimal prices. She thinks that nowadays the Arabs are well-advised as to what an animal is worth, and they pay the right price.

Within the industry, everyone experiences both good and bad times. Horse racing has become big business, and Sonia maintains that there is less fun to be had nowadays, as the figures are so large and the vets have to be extremely cautious. In her opinion, vets are frightened to sign off on anything, but there is no such thing as perfection. She would not agree with any suggestion that the industry is any more corrupt than any other. You've got to learn your trade and watch yourself, she says.

Her role in the industry

Sonia is quietly proud of the fact that she became the first female member of the Turf Club. This was in 1985, on Lord Hemphill's watch, which she finds ironic because he believed women should not be involved! Sonia has also served on the Racing Board and on the Board of Navan Racecourse. Currently, she is a director at Goffs. She remarks that these are thankless jobs and there is no salary. The industry is dominated by men, although Sonia believes that there are other very competent women who should occupy positions as directors. She praises the work of the Turf Club which she believes gets inadequate recognition, and whose stewards perform a difficult role for which they are not paid.

The future

Sonia Rogers believes the future is bright while John Magnier is at Coolmore producing good stallions, Khalid Abdullah has great mares here, and Aidan O'Brien wins big races in England. She hopes that the Irish National Stud continues to function, as she maintains that the Irish breed the best horses in the world, and also the best horse men and women. No matter where one goes in the world, Irish men and women will be working with horses. Ireland has wonderful jockeys, fine horsemen who learn horsemanship at a young age.

In Sonia's opinion, people tend not to realise the great importance of the horse to Ireland, though she believes that the present Minister for Agriculture, Simon Coveney, is indeed alert to this. Money is needed for investment to update the racecourses, she says; the horses are brilliant but they are not showcased well.

Rogers' stud is a thriving and successful business, now in the hands of the second generation of the family. The stud extends to over 400 acres, with another 300 acres in Simmonstown. Sonia believes it is very important to know when the time has come to make the decision to hand over control to a younger person, as she did. She has learnt quite a lot from her son, particularly in the area of technology, but to an equal extent he continues to learn from his mother's vast experience. ■

Sonia Rogers.

Barbara Collins with Very Proud.

CHAPTER 20

BARBARA COLLINS

" Jack Doyle once said: He [the horse] doesn't
know he only cost 5,000 guineas! **"**

Barbara Collins begins by recalling "the brilliant life" she has had with horses and the horse-racing world, and she declares that she has been fortunate enough to meet the nicest people during that time.

Dublin-born Barbara Collins married into the world of racing. Born in the late 1930s, she was brought up with no experience of horses, though her father did bring her to race meetings at nearby Phoenix Park and at the Curragh. She went to school at Loretto College, St Stephen's Green, and later began work at Brown Thomas. At 18 she met her future husband, Con Collins, at a dinner in the Shelbourne Hotel, when both of them were seated at the top table. Due to Barbara's work commitments, it was some time before they got together. At 21 years of age, she began to work for Switzers, in a position which required her to travel all over Europe, to places such as Paris and Milan. At the age of 24, Barbara married Con and they made their home in the Curragh, where she has now lived for almost fifty years. Con passed away in 2007 at the age of 82.

Move to the Curragh

Prior to their marriage, Con Collins lived in his own house, Melitta Lodge, and his parents lived at Conyngham Lodge where Con had been reared from the age of six. His father M. C. (Mick) Collins died in 1961 and Con bought the property from the family. It is a source of great regret to Barbara that she never knew her father-in-law.

Conyngham Lodge was named for the family now based at Slane Castle. In the past, Conyngham Hall had stood close by, and when a daughter of the family married, Conyngham Lodge and stables, were built for her and her husband. The Hall has now gone. Con's father Mick was there since early 1930s, but previously there had been trainers resident there too. One of them was Captain Joy, who may have been a relation of the original Conynghams. Barbara named one of her horses Captain Joy which was trained by her daughter, to their delight it won at Dundalk in December 2011.

When Barbara arrived at Conyngham Lodge, she thought that it was the "coldest house in Europe" and that the Curragh was the bleakest place, but within a year her view had changed. She had learned how to ride, not well, as she says herself, but well enough and she had become involved with the business end of the stables, in what would now be known as public relations. She reckons that in the last twenty years she has gone to Dublin perhaps twice a year. One of the first people she met when she came to Conyngham Lodge was Mickey Shanahan. In all her time there he has never missed a Saturday morning and has gone to every race meeting that they have had a runner. He is a very important part of the Collins' family.

Barbara recalls that in earlier days, there were no railings on the Curragh. Apparently the Curragh is a commonage and various local people have sheep rights; so that for every sheep right which exists, two sheep can be grazed. Barbara herself has 67 sheep rights today. When the idea of railing in the Curragh Racecourse was suggested, a group of people got together to pool their sheep rights, so that the corresponding ground could be railed. However, sheep still run out, so there are sheep traps on the stables entrance. When a horse drops its rider on the Curragh, Barbara explains, the animal knows where to come into the yard, as the entrance to the Curragh is just across the road from the stables.

During the half-century in which Barbara has been living on the Curragh, she has met most of the people in the industry. Amongst the first were Bill Harrington (or more formally William Stanhope, 11th Earl Harrington), who was a very good friend of Con Collins. He died three years ago, and Barbara describes him as one of the nicest men she has ever met. Barney Eastwood and Alfie McLean (who passed away in 2006) were bookmakers whom Barbara describes as absolutely delightful people. These three people were the first owners she met, and all three are listed in the early pages of a book listing Con's winners.

Conyngham Lodge Stables

Barbara is proud to describe her husband's "fantastic success". Out of the 50 to 60 horses he trained yearly, he won four Group 1 races and many Group 2 and Group 3 races. He had a great and consuming passion for the sport.

Con Collins had established himself as a trainer before his marriage. Barbara recalls that he was a great judge of a horse, who could actually buy horses quite cheaply because he was mostly interested in the look of the horse and its breeding, and he did not mind if the sire was not fashionable. He bought horses from Goffs, Tattersalls, Newmarket and so on, but Barbara explains that there was not a great number of horses around because the market was not as sophisticated as it is today. She recalls that before their marriage, Con bought two horses which he had seen in a field when he was passing by, for an Englishman named Schofield. These horses proved to be very successful indeed.

Part of Barbara's role in earlier days at Conyngham Lodge stables was to bring in new owners, and she organised parties for the owners and everyone else in the racing world to this end. People such as Victor and Beryl McCalmont were included, and while Victor was Senior Steward, and perhaps Beryl felt disinclined to attend an event in the Turf Club, he would drop her off at one of the Collinses' parties at Conyngham Lodge. The parties would also be attended by people from Tattersalls, and many English owners. Barbara recalls the great friendliness and camaraderie which existed between all sections of the horse-racing industry: the owners, the trainers and the jockeys. Con Collins and Charlie Weld were great friends though in the same business. The money was not the same as it is now but they all survived, says Barbara. The business has become much more commercial, but a certain horse will always bring in a big crowd, she continues.

The care of the racehorses is the primary concern of the trainer and his staff. The horses are never left out alone, unless into the paddock, and even then an eye must be kept on them. All horses are treated exactly the same, whatever their value. Barbara smiles as she recalls what Jack Doyle once said: "He [the horse] didn't know he only cost 5,000 guineas!"

A question arises relating to the qualities required in a good trainer. In Barbara's opinion, one had to be brought up with horses and have a passion for them. You must know about horses – Con was always right instinctively, she says, about what was wrong with a horse – "the vets only had seven years in college!" In addition, the placing of a horse in a race was crucial to its success. Placing refers to putting the horse in the appropriate race for it to have the greatest chance of winning. It involves judging the distance or length of the race, the ground, and whether the course is right- or left-handed to suit the horse and finally, but very importantly, the competition. In Barbara's opinion Con had a real skill at placing his horses. She adjudges that Mark Prescott in England, for instance, is also brilliant at placing horses.

Over the years Con and Barbara never had more than fifty or sixty horses, and they employed about sixteen to twenty-one staff. They had twenty-eight acres on the Curragh and another one hundred and twenty acres about a mile away. Con managed the land, and he loved the fields and the cattle – he was a great farmer. As Barbara explains, most trainers would be knowledgeable about the land and farming as well as about horses.

The Collins stable mainly trained horses for the Flat. However, Con also trained the three times Champion Hurdler See You Then, and he won six races with him, four on the Flat and two over hurdles. The owner was Alfie McLean, who was offered such good money for him that he could not refuse to sell him. If a trainer or an owner gets a good price, it's good fortune. One is always sad to see a horse go, but there is no money in training a horse, and as Barbara points out, you also get a lot of bad ones mixed in with the few good ones.

Barbara declares that her husband thought of nothing else but his horses, to the extent that he never thought about the money and just signed the cheques! It was Barbara's task to look after the finances.

The only time that Barbara heard Con say that he was going to win a race was when he placed Princess Pati in the 1984 Irish Oaks with Pat Shanahan on board – and he was right! However, as Barbara is very much aware, there are many slips on the day over which a trainer has no control.

Meetings in Tralee

After her marriage, one of the first meetings Barbara attended was at Tralee, which was to become one of her favourite meets. At that meeting, one of the winners was a horse owned by solicitor Joe Grace. After that they went to Tralee every year during the Rose of Tralee festival and would stay for two nights over the three-day meeting. There was always a great atmosphere there. Galway was only really starting then, Barbara recalls, and today there are seven days

> **"** When I arrived at Conyngham Lodge I thought it was the coldest house in Europe! **"**

of racing in Galway and none at all in Tralee. She recalls that over the years Galway, Listowel, Tralee and Killarney were great meetings to go to with great excitement, but the races were very competitive. Of course, a lot of work was involved in preparing the horses, putting them into the boxes and travelling on roads that are not as good as they are now. Over the days of an event, not all the horses would travel at the same time, as some would go the day before, some would go one day and come back the next, and so on.

The jockeys at the stables

One marvellous jockey in the stables at Conyngham Lodge was Pat Shanahan from Tipperary. When Pat was 15 years of age, his father phoned Con about a place for him. Con's uncle in Cork would sometimes send up young fellows on the train to work at the stables. For five years, they would stay in dormitories in the stables, be fed and get a wage. Barbara would not so much 'mother' them as take responsibility for them, as she explains that, after all, someone had sent their child to you and they had to be looked after. She says that they had to do what they were told, and still today, when she goes to the Curragh, the now older men say 'Hello Ma'am' or 'Yes Ma'am' when they meet her. Out of the many apprentice jockeys, there were some very good individuals such as Mark Lynch, who became European Champion apprentice.

Lord Dunraven (far right) with an unidentified jockey and friends at the races.

Golf outing with Flor Burke (2nd from left), M. C. Collins (2nd from right), Seán Lemass (right). *Irish Press.*

Barbara Collins

Roderick More O'Ferrall (left), M. C. Collins (centre) and
Roderick's brother (seated).

Others might have got too heavy, or have left for England. Barbara calls to mind an emotional visit from a man who was an apprentice for Con's father and who later worked for Con himself. He had travelled to Conyngham Lodge from the far side of Limerick to pay his respects after Con's death. He said it had been forty years since he had last been in the house. The connections stay strong, and run very deep.

Some of the apprentices would stay on to work in the yard. Barbara recalls one such apprentice who was nicknamed "Goofy", who had worked in the yard since he was 10 years of age. She made sure he went to school, but when he turned 14 he refused to return to his education. Sadly he died in 2002 at the age of 42 in a car accident which happened just down the road from the yard.

It is a well-known fact that a jockey sustains many injuries during his working life. Con's father, Mick Collins, along with others including Joe McGrath, set up the 'jockey hospital' on the Curragh, reasoning that an injured jockey could be put into a car and taken there for care by the local doctor who decided what needed to be done. About forty years ago, operations were also undertaken there. The Drogheda Memorial Hospital – familiarly known as the 'Jockey Hospital' was named after Henry Moore, 3rd Marquess of Drogheda – was built about 1894 on the edge of the Curragh. Con Collins, continuing the family connection, was on the committee of the Drogheda Memorial Fund until he died.

Today, many women work in the horse racing industry and as Barbara points out they are becoming a big part of the business. They include her own daughters Sheena and Tracey. Barbara recalls Helen O'Sullivan and Joanna Morgan who were the first two female riders, and she says that Helen was a very good apprentice for Con. Barbara herself, of course, was involved in running the business, like many other trainers' wives, and as she reflects back, she says that Con did what he knew best and he left her do what she did best. Barbara, in tribute to her late husband, that he treated everyone the same no matter what position they held, or which gender they were. He was "a total gentleman", she says.

Times have changed

Barbara has fond memories of many people involved in the horse industry, including stud-owner Tony Tarry, now 86, Victor McCalmont of the Turf Club, John de Burgh of the Irish Racing Board, the trainers 'Darkie' Prendergast and Vincent O'Brien, and Peter Patrick Hemphill, Lord Hemphill. These men, she says, were completely dedicated to horses and often worked on a voluntary basis. Naturally, these wonderful personalities would clash sometimes but this all added to the colour and zest of the racing world. That world has become very commercial nowadays, she continues, and has quite a different emphasis.

She recalls that there were fewer races in the early days, and a race was never held on a Sunday. This suited the Collins family very well – it was their only day off. Every Sunday, Barbara would host lunch at 3 p.m., and it became an 'open house' where visitors were welcome. The Collinses always tried to let everybody off for four days at Christmas. This meant that with their three daughters, Con and Barbara looked after the horses, with the help of anybody who was staying over for the holiday. Christmas dinner would be around 6 p.m. after all the work was done. Today, it is a seven-day-a-week business.

A risky business

Barbara feels that it is wonderful that people are able to make money from racing nowadays, in comparison to the situation in the past. However, she has great sympathy for young trainers in the early stages, as it is difficult to find owners, and some may not pay. In order to get a start, a trainer has to have owners with friends and relatives to begin with. Horse racing is a luxury and very expensive. In addition to their fees, owners are advised to insure their horses. However, many, if not most, owners will not do this, and when something happens, that is it. It is a tough world and tough decisions have to be made, she says.

She has seen good and bad days in the business. One year, about 32 years ago, Barbara recalls that they had just two winners. Then she went to London with two of her friends to see Frank Sinatra perform, at a time before mobile phones were in use. At the hotel a man came up to her and said, "You had a great day today." "What do you mean?", she said. He replied, "You won two two-year old races!" On the next evening while travelling home, another man approached her at the airport and told her how they had again won two two-year old races that day. So that marked the end of a long losing streak!

If money was made in a season, it would be spent on whatever was needed, and then the cycle started all over again. Once Con bought seventy acres and then an adjoining sixty acres, and that became the site of the stud farm. And then, as Barbara reminds us, the next year there might be no money at all. Today, deep in a recession, things are difficult for everybody, "but we will get over it", she says, with quiet confidence.

Gambling and bookmakers

Some of the horse owners at Conyngham Lodge stables were bookmakers, and Barbara recalls such people as Barney Eastwood, Alfie McLean, for whom Con won a Group 1 race in England with Sandy Creek, and at one time, J. P. McManus. Con had J. P.'s first winners.

Barbara is not particularly interested in betting, and she remarks that Con would bet only three times a year, to her knowledge. In all the years, only once did all three bets lose! A trainer can do everything to make things right but, on the day, something can happen which is out of one's own control. One single occasion on which she placed a bet was at a time when William Hill, the English bookmaker and a great friend of theirs, came to stay. Barbara tells us that she overheard him saying to her young daughter, "I think your mummy's horse is going to win today." Barbara then asked him whether he really thought that was true. He said he did and then he urged her to put a bet on, to which she replied that she did not bet. Eventually William Hill persuaded her to put £50 on, and a few days later she got a cheque with her winnings for nearly £500! She couldn't believe it, but she still was not tempted to continue betting!

The favourite

Barbara's favourite horse – The Bower – was a very special animal that Con had bought as a yearling. He ran a number of times as a two- and three-year old. The Bower won at Bellewstown as a three-year old. From then on he raced 42 times, won 13 times and only once was not placed in the first three of all of these races. He went from a rating of 42 to 105.

No guarantees – a tough business

The Collins family of Conyngham Lodge have had many owners over the years, and now work with the succeeding generation. Among them are Alfie McLean (who died six years ago, but his son has a horse at the stables today) and Bill Harrington (who passed away three years ago), Frank Hardy, a Steward of the Turf Club had horses with Con from the time he practically started. Frank had a lot of group winners but, unfortunately, he is now deceased. Clody Norton's father, Bobby Hall-Dare had horses with Conyngham Lodge Stables, she still has and also her family. As Barbara says, "We keep our owners but you have to get new owners in".

Barbara's daughters Sheena, Tracey and Natalie worked with their father Con since childhood. Natalie took a different path but is still very much involved in the horses. She has a restaurant at the National Stud and the Silver Restaurant at Newbridge Silverware. Sheena and Tracey became Con's assistants from an early age. Sheena became a trainer in her own right alongside her father. She trained group winners and was very successful. She now has two daughters who look like they will follow in their mother's footsteps. Tracey now trains at Conyngham Lodge and she too has trained group winners. Barbara is very proud of them all. Their father's fine skill at spotting a good horse seems to have been passed on to them, as Barbara tells of an incident when Con was ill towards the end of his life. He was unable to go to the sales and the girls rang him up to say they had seen a horse that they really liked. Con told them to follow their instinct so Chelsea Rose came home. Chelsea Rose won the Group 1 Moyglare Group Stakes in 2004. They continued their father's success with Dandy Man who is now a sire.

The future looks bright at Conyngham Lodge Stables with another Collins at the helm. ∎

Bill Harrington (left) having a laugh with Con Collins.

Betty Galway-Greer at a Hunt Ball.

CHAPTER 21

BETTY GALWAY-GREER

" I was probably put sitting up on a
horse before I could walk, and then my father bought a
Shetland pony for me. **"**

PROFILE

Betty
Galway-Greer

Rooske Lodge
Dunboyne
Co. Meath

Born:
1930s

Occupation:
Breeder

Rooske Lodge has been home to Betty Galway-Greer all through her life. Her parents, Nat Galway-Greer and Gladys Lawlor, bought the property during the war years, and further adjoining land was added over time.

Nat's father, a farmer, had little interest in horses apart from work horses. Nat, however, loved horses from an early age, buying his first horse when he was just fourteen years old, using a loan from his mother. He prepared this horse and took it to a local show, where it won first prize; the horse that took second had been a champion in Dublin! With an enduring passion for horses, he would cycle anywhere to meetings, often to Baldoyle or to Punchestown.

He loved showing horses, hunting and racing, but had no particular interest in showjumping. He was also an amateur jockey but, at 6' 2½" he had difficulty maintaining the appropriate weight. His daughter Betty remarks that apparently his party trick in the weigh room was to take off his old-fashioned collar, and to button it around his waist!

Gladys Lawlor, Betty's mother, came from Irishtown, Clondalkin in Dublin. Though Gladys herself did not ride, her sisters enjoyed it, and one of them was considered to be a very good showjumper. Betty's aunt Oonagh married J. E. Ryan, who was well known as an amateur point to pointer and who became a top National Hunt trainer in the USA. Gladys' role in the family stud farm business was to entertain visitors, and Betty recalls her mother's regret that she had not kept a visitors' book down through the years, as people had come from all over the world to buy horses. Betty recalls that her father was very hospitable, and that everyone would be invited to the house.

Betty's interests

Betty was educated as a day pupil at Loreto College on Stephen's Green, Dublin. She loved Dunboyne, and the life there, and being surrounded by horses. Her first horse was a Shetland pony bought for her by her father Nat, and she later graduated to a pony for hunting with the North Kildare Harriers. Nat always ensured that Betty had really good hunters; she has fond memories of Two Ticks, a grey thoroughbred. However, she knew her own limitations as a rider, she says, and thinks perhaps that as an only child she was not sufficiently competitive. When Betty was quite young, her mother gave her a filly, Crenella, out of Cowrie by Luminary. Crenella was trained by Charlie Weld and won a two-year old race at Baldoyle racecourse. She was subsequently placed in a few good races, and from her Betty bred a number of winners. Another successful horse for Betty was Refined, given to her by her father. She was bought as a little woolly foal, sired by Abadan and later sold as a yearling to Paddy 'Darkie' Prendergast, and she was the best two- and three-year old filly in Ireland and England at that time. Refined won the 1956 Phoenix Stakes at the Phoenix Park and also a number of races in England.

Betty reflects on the challenges involved in the naming of a horse, as even when a few names are submitted, they might already have been assigned. The name of Refined, daughter of Abadan, came from the oil refinery in Abadan, Iran. With this in mind, and thinking of Cowrie, Betty went on a research trip to the National Library in Dublin where she studied a book on molluscs. She noted the names of different types of molluscs such as *Caprella* and *Crenella* which were subsequently used for the descendants of Cowrie.

Betty has many and varied memories, and she notes the many changes which have taken place over time. She remembers the Phoenix Park races as a lovely event, with punters travelling out from Dublin city. The old parade ring was very sociable, she says, as people circulated easily from the stand to the ring. She recalls women who hunted sidesaddle, and her mother told her about her two sisters who fought hard to the finish of a point to point, one sister riding sidesaddle and the other astride! Another change which has occurred is the fact that point to points did not have brush fences as now; participants jumped from one field to another over the wall, fence or ditch which was in their way, over a distance of about three miles.

The business

The Galway-Greer family were in the business of selling horses, either bred on the farm or sourced around the country for clients in Ireland and abroad. For instance, Gladys's mare Cowrie had a filly named Cockle who, after being sold as a yearling, went on to win two Norwegian classic races. Betty recalls that her father Nat would travel anywhere in the country to find the sort of horse he was seeking. He relied on his own opinion of a horse, having once asked a vet to look at a three-year old thoroughbred. The vet reported that he did not like its legs, so Nat decided not to buy the horse – that was Easter Hero, twice winner of the Cheltenham Gold Cup! From then on, he examined the horses himself, which worked out well. As one farmer said, if Nat looked at a horse and then decided not to buy, no-one else was any the wiser, but if the vet gave a horse a negative rating, then everyone would know. Once Nat had decided to buy, he paid by cheque and the horse was put on the train to Clonsilla. Betty believes he was a very good judge of a horse and could look at a foal and evaluate its likely future. His sound reputation and credibility were built up through recommendations and word of mouth, and Betty says that he was honourable and would not sell a horse to a buyer if he thought the horse would not suit that person; they would be directed to another animal.

The challenge of remaining in business during wartime was evident to Betty as a child. She recalls Nat's efforts to keep cattle and to ship them to England which was suffering from food shortages, and also to stock sheep. Even then there were always horses about the place. Nat went into bloodstock breeding after the war in a small way. This meant buying fillies and putting them to stud or buying foals in Newmarket and selling them as yearlings the following year. The National Hunt horses would be three- or four-year olds when Nat bought them, and they were mainly sold on to English buyers for racing.

Among the prestigious horses to pass through Nat's hands was Golden Miller, by Gold Court, out of Miller's Pride, bred near Dunshaughlin by Laurence Geraghty and then sold as a yearling at Goffs during Horse Show Week. Nat had already had two of its half-brothers and was anxious to buy this yearling, but he just missed the sale. He offered to buy him from the new owner who declined the offer. When the horse turned three, Nat again offered to buy him and this time he succeeded. Nat then received a telegram from England asking if he could source the best prospective three-year old chaser in Ireland, and he replied, "He's in the yard". Golden Miller went on to win five Cheltenham Gold Cups in succession from 1932 to 1936, and the Aintree Grand National in 1934. He is the most successful Gold Cup winner, and the only horse to win both a Gold Cup and Grand National in the same year.

Other famous horses were Amber Point and Knight Errant, which were own brothers and were sold to Ann Biddle. They were trained by Paddy Sleator. Amber Point went on to win fourteen races, including the Galway Plate in 1954 and 1956, while Knight Errant won nine races, including the Galway Plate in 1957 and the 1958 Galway Hurdle. Another Flash, Poor Flame, Workboy and many others were also very successful.

Nat Galway-Greer and Tom Dreaper enjoyed a longstanding friendship. The Dreaper stables were not far away in Greenogue and, as Betty recalls, nearly every Sunday they would discuss the horses of interest and the racing issues of the day. Tom trained a few horses for Nat, as also did Paddy Sleator and Vincent O'Brien.

Showing horses

Nat Galway-Greer always showed horses at the Dublin Horse Show at the RDS. Betty remembers that visitors came from all over the world for Horse Show week in August, as this is a prestigious event which offers a showcase of Irish horses. Nat won many trophies at the RDS. One was the Laidlaw Cup, which had been presented by his great friend T. K. Laidlaw to the RDS in 1926. Nat won this as Supreme Champion for three years in succession, in 1947 to 1949, and thus was entitled to retain the trophy. Another trophy he also won in perpetuity was the Bright Prospect Trophy, which was in the form of a tray and was awarded to the Supreme Champion.

Nat was an accomplished rider in his day. He owned winning Supreme Champions on ten occasions, the first was with Mighty Fine in 1947, then Mighty Atom in 1948, Splendour in 1949, then four years in a row from 1957-1960, and again three times in the early 1960s. Betty remarks that it had been won three times in a row previously, but always with the same horse. Nat was the first person to win with ten individual horses. Unfortunately, in 1956 Nat was to suffer serious injuries following a fall under a horse, and he was hospitalised for many weeks. After his recovery, he could ride but with discomfort, though did not show it because of his stoical nature.

Nat did not retire, but Betty believes that his constant smoking eventually damaged his health. He suffered a stroke and was admitted to the Mater Hospital. However, he insisted on coming home to supervise the farrier a few days before the Dublin Horse Show. He then went back to hospital and suffered another slight stroke. Despite this, he made a good recovery, though

> " Nat got a telegram from England about sourcing the best prospective three-year-old chaser in Ireland. "He's in the yard", he replied. "

his vision was affected and he could no longer drive which was distressing for him, as he could no longer get about all over the country sourcing horses as before. Nat Galway-Greer died in October 1974, and his wife Gladys passed away in 1977.

Betty Galway-Greer maintains that breeding and rearing horses is a lot of hard work, and success also depends on luck. After her father's death, it became necessary for her to take over the business. The times were not favourable in the 1970s, due to the oil crisis. Heretofore, the yearling market had been good, but then the economy contracted which affected the yearling market. Betty sent five yearlings to Newmarket, where only two were sold, though she recalls that some people were unable to sell any horses, and for a period of time expenses were not being covered even if horses were sold. The situation did improve after a time, and Betty was managing the business as well as was possible, though a great amount of change and transition had occurred in a short time.

Betty is proud to say that today horses can still be traced back to Rooske breeding, for example Legal Exit, which won a point to point in 2012, and Xinbama, winner of flat races in England also in 2012. The fine Galway-Greer family legacy lives on. ∎

Crenella winning at Baldoyle. *The Irish Times*.

In the winners' enclosure at Baldoyle: jockey Peter Connelly, Betty's aunt, Dodo Lawlor, beside Nat Galway-Greer (extreme right).

Tom Dreaper (left) and Nat Galway-Greer. *The Irish Times*.

Mighty Atom at the 1948 Cork Show with Nat Galway-Greer.

Johnny Kierans.

CHAPTER 22

JOHNNY KIERANS

" Mick McGuinness also bred the great Galloway Braes for the late Lord Harrington. "

PROFILE

Johnny Kierans

Drogheda
Co. Louth

Born:
1939

Occupation:
Compositor

Having come from a family of painters, bakers, barbers and hairdressers, Johnny Kierans 'escaped' to the world of printing as a youth in Drogheda. While growing up, he helped out in his father's barber shop where one of his jobs was to place bets for customers at Richard Powers, the bookmaker's next door. Miss Gemma Power, daughter of Dick Power, was in charge there in the 1950s, and she is now in her nineties. Johnny recalls that he won all seven prizes, including the two prizes in maths, in 6th class at school, and he utilised his mathematical skills in making up the bets in the back room of the bookmakers on Grand National day.

When he was 14 he left school and, and he clearly remembers the day – May 10 1954 – when he became an apprentice compositor at the *Drogheda Independent*. There he worked in the general jobbing section with Andrew Belton (design compositor) and Tom O'Donoghue (compositor), both top-notch tradesmen and also keen racegoers who brought the young man along with them to the races. Johnny had already been introduced to racing by his father, also named John, who attended Bellewstown races regularly, accompanied by all the family. In the early days, nobody had cars, so the family would travel in a hired taxi to the races. Thus, Johnny attended his first race meeting at the age of 3, and he continues his long tradition of attendance at Bellewstown, having recently gone there for the 69th time.

Johnny remembers great days at the races with Andrew and Tom, as a young man. He recalls seeing Eamon Delaney winning the bumper at Naas on Rare Toy. Other horses he recalls from that time were Caherdaniel bred by one of his father's customers, Mick McGuinness from Ballywalter just outside Drogheda. This horse was trained by Charlie Chute in Kerry for the late Lord Harrington. Mick McGuinness also bred the great Galloway Braes, which won the 1953 King George VI Stakes at Kempton Park on Boxing Day.

Horse racing and greyhounds

Johnny has a great memory for the names of horses and for various details of a race, such as the odds. He tells an anecdote about a horse of J. F. Hoey's which was sent to Haydock Park and ridden by Mickey Beary. The odds on the horse were 20/1 with the favourite being odds on at 2/5. It was ridden by Gordon Richards (later Sir Gordon). Johnny's father was backing the horse in Ireland along with some others. Although they were very confident, the horse stumbled 100 yards from the line and went down. Johnny's father used to say the message to be learned was that there was no such thing as a certainty. Johnny recalls that there were a lot of dubious practices in racing at that time, but that they are almost gone now and certainly not as prevalent as they were fifty or sixty years ago. He himself could never afford to bet heavily, and he says his first real bet would have been in 1990.

Both Johnny and his father owned greyhounds. In the early 1960s Johnny won a trial stake in Killucan with Una's Pleasure, the first bitch he had ever run. There were many other wins as well. Along with training greyhounds, Johnny has also written about them since he was about 15 or 16 years of age, with articles in the *Irish Independent, Irish Press* and *Sporting Press*.

Working in the printing business

Having served his time at the *Drogheda Independent* for seven years, Johnny was appointed overseer in the general jobbing section of the newspaper. He married Carmel Halpin in 1961, when they were both aged 22, and they had seven children. His next position in his working life was that of foreman, looking after the *Drogheda Independent*, the *Drogheda Argus*, the *Dundalk Argus*, and also the books printed at the works. At this stage, his former mentor Andrew Belton had become works manager.

At that time, the *Drogheda Independent* were printing racecards, and Johnny designed a new type of racecard in early 1960. He changed the shape of the originally square-shaped card to that of a longer format, which was easier to produce, and which also fitted conveniently into a pocket. To make the cards, he had purchased a Double Crown machine second-hand in England, and it had hoppers which reduced the manual labour required. It folded one sheet into 24 pages, and only required a cover at the end of the process.

The works were printing racecards for the racecourses at Bellewstown, Dundalk, Phoenix Park and Mullingar amongst others, and also cards for the local Baymore point to point and Mullacurry point to point. They did not print racecards for any of the major racecourses such as Leopardstown in those days.

The racecards

Johnny explains the process of producing racecards at that time, which serves to illuminate the practices of sixty years ago. The Clerk of the Course was responsible for the accuracy of the racecard. The copy would be supplied to the printers in handwritten form with the following information: the number, the form lines (indicating where the horse had finished in the previous three races), the horse's name, its breeding, the name of the owner and trainer, and the weight. At that stage the jockey's name was not included on the racecard. This information was sent in to the printer about five or six days before the race meeting. It was set up in linotype, and then the proofs from the galley press were sent to the Turf Club for checking. In those days, there were two-day declarations. Then, the racecourse would ring up with the names of the declared horses, the non-runners would be removed by the printers, the card was set up again and read back over the phone by the printers. Johnny recalls that in the late 1960s, Irish Racing Services was set up by Christy Glennon and Noel Reid, and they then supplied the names of jockeys for the racecards. The printers would ring Irish Racing Services at an appointed time to get the jockeys' names, they would then make up pages of the racecard, page them, lay them out in the chase, insert margins and so on.

At this stage, Johnny's knowledge of the track would come into play. He says that often there would be a division and he would ring up with corrections, the Turf Club would check it out and amendments would be made as appropriate.

In an interesting aside, Johnny recalls that the numbers of the horses would be assigned in the Turf Club. At one time, they were set depending on weight; if all were at level weights then the number would be set in alphabetical order on the card.

A section of the crowd in the main grandstand at Bellewstown Races in 1915. Some British Army personnel can be seen amongst the punters.

Innovations in printing

In 1970, Johnny was sent to Kodak in High Holborn, London, to do a week-long course in graphic arts in black and white and colour, during which he stayed in a hotel in Piccadilly. When he returned home, the *Drogheda Independent* was set up with offset printing which used film, an innovative technology at the time. However, the racecards were still being produced using hot metal. Following his return, Johnny wrote a report on these new developments, including offset printing, to the directors of the *Drogheda Independent*, though he recalls that the report was not implemented until the 1990s. In any event, the printing works were taken over by Tony O'Reilly's private company, and Johnny notes that O'Reilly was the son of a Drogheda man. The titles later became part of the Independent Group of newspapers.

Setting up Anglo Printers

Following the sale, Johnny recalls that many problems arose between management in Dublin and the unions, and that he found himself in a difficult position between the two. Eventually he made the decision to leave in the early 1980s. At this stage, he was working as sales and marketing manager, and he recalls that on the day he gave in his notice, he went out to work as usual and brought home about £25,000 of business. He then went home for a late lunch, and one of the van

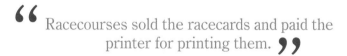

" Racecourses sold the racecards and paid the printer for printing them. "

drivers called to his door to say that he had been sent for the keys of the car. Despite this, Johnny went back to the office, worked out his notice and then handed back the keys. Next he bought a new car for himself and set up his own business, Elite Print.

Within twelve months, the jobbing printing section of the *Drogheda Independent* had closed. Johnny relates that when he took over as sales and marketing manager at the newspaper, they were doing business valued at about £150,000 a year, and at the time of his departure, that figure had increased to £500,000. He reasoned that if he could do it for that business, he could it for himself. and he is very glad that he took the decision to work for himself. He was backed in his new business by Brendan Kelly and his brother Ronan (grandsons of Joe McGrath), who put £20,000 into the business. Johnny recalls that Brendan and Ronan were very good directors who regularly attended meetings. Gerard Magee of Haughey Boland was the accountant for the business. Johnny then went off to England to buy second-hand machinery, and his first commission was for the printing of the racecard for Leopardstown racecourse. The course was managed by Frank Smith who was also secretary of the Racing Board, and who Johnny describes as one of the greatest administrators Ireland has ever known. (Johnny also pays credit to Smith's team of Tony Corcoran and Tom Burke and chairman Paddy Walsh, and he declares that it took what is now Horse Racing Ireland to replace those fine men.)

Anglo Printers finishing department, 1983.

Listowel Race Card, 1964.

John Kierans pictured with famous jockey Lester Piggott at Bellewstown races in 2011. Also pictured are Peter and Pádraic Kierans of Anglo Printers.

Anglo Printers celebrate their first win at Fairyhouse with winner Kilbyrne King. Pictured are Pádraic Kierans (left), John Kierans, jockey Denis Leahy, groom Brendan Walsh, Peter Kierans and Joe Walsh.

In order to get business, Johnny pursued the production, by his company, of all the racecards. Historically, they had been produced by Brindleys in Dublin. Over time, most of the racecourses realised that Brindleys were making a large profit from the production of the racecards, and the racecourses were not benefitting. The business was transferred to Anglo Printers who offered competitive rates, and from then onwards, the racecourses sold the racecards, and contracted the printers. Leopardstown was the first racecourse for which he produced racecards, then Bellewstown, and on it went. Johnny was the first printer to include the jockeys' silks in colour on racecards, initially for the Curragh, Phoenix Park and Leopardstown. During the recession of the 1980s, Johnny recalls that he really had to work hard to get the business.

The Racing Board had been producing an annual racing calendar and a diary, produced by Smurfits until that company closed the publishing arm of their business. In 1983, Johnny got the rights for Anglo Printers to produce the calendar, and since then, the Irish Racing Calendar has been produced by Anglo Printers.

Further innovations

Always a person of innovative thinking, Johnny designed the first Tote duplicate ticket. This was made of two parts: paper on which were written the numbers, with a card underneath, which the punter kept to make a claim. He was then approached by the late Ted Curtin and Peter McCreery, chairman and secretary of the Irish Racehorse Trainers Association, who enquired if he could do overnight declarations to replace the two-day declaration then in operation. Always the businessman, Johnny replied that it might be slightly more expensive because of overtime, but that it was possible. Thus, he became the first man to produce a racecard overnight. The big advantage for trainers was that the intervening time between declared horses and the race meeting was greatly shortened.

Another innovation introduced by Johnny was a 'Best Dressed Lady' competition at Bellewstown racecourse, though there it was called the 'Most Appropriately Dressed Lady' competition. Anglo Printers sponsored the competition and Johnny's sons now continue the tradition to this day. Such competitions are held at most race meetings today, and they attract large numbers and some very valuable publicity.

Retirement from printing

In 1996 Johnny was advised by his doctors to retire, as the pressure of business was taking its toll. He had started his business during a recession, and had laboured long and hard over many years. He recalls that at one stage he owed Revenue Commissioners about a quarter of a million pounds, and he also owed a paper supplier a similar amount, but he is glad to be able to say that by the time he retired, he had cleared all the business debts. On his retirement, he sold the business in two equal shares to his two sons, Pádraic and Peter, and they continue to run the company to this day.

It is fair to say that Johnny Kierans can look back, with quiet pride, on a long life of innovation and progress. ■

German printing engineer, the late Horst Rautenberg, pictured on the opening day of Anglo Printers Ltd, in 1983 with founder John Kierans.

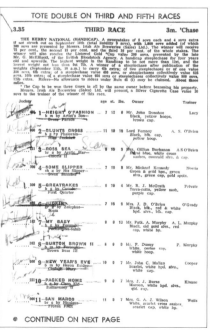

Listowel Race Card, detail showing runners in the Kerry National chase.

Elite Print and Local News stand with founder, John Kierans, at the Commercial Exhibition in the Star and Crescent recreation centre, Drogheda, in 1980.

Valentine Lamb.

CHAPTER 23

VALENTINE LAMB

❝ I always wanted to get hold of the *Irish Field*, so going
to the *Irish Times* was really a stepping stone. ❞

Valentine Lamb was born in the small village of Coombe Bisset in Wiltshire, the son of portrait painter Henry Lamb, and a peer's daughter. His father had left home and, against family wishes, had become a painter. He was later to qualify as a doctor and served in this capacity in the British Army. For his services during the First World War and in Palestine he was awarded the Military Cross, but, after the horrors of war, had had enough of medicine, so he began to paint full-time. Valentine's mother was Lady Pansy Pakenham, daughter of Lord Longford. The Irish home of the Pakenhams was Pakenham Hall (now known as Tullynally) in Castlepollard, County Westmeath, where Valentine often stayed during his childhood.

Valentine went to prep school in Salisbury Cathedral School, famed for its cathedral choir, though he remarks that owing to his non-existent singing voice, he became official page-turner for the music master! At 14, he attended King's Bruton School in Somerset and, not being particularly academic, he got employment immediately afterwards. His first job as a mundane clerk was at Lloyd's Bank in Salisbury, and two years later he was called up for National Service in the Air Force. He recalls with amusement an occasion, while square bashing, when the drill sergeant shouted an inch from his face: "your mother wanted a girl, your father wanted a boy and they were both disappointed!"

Later he answered an advertisement for a job with the *Financial Times* in London, as "financial statistician" – and was accepted. This was a clerical post, he explains. Throughout the years, his greatest wish was to live in Ireland and when he did manage a visit, he first stayed with his uncle and aunt at Pakenham Hall. During one visit he read a copy of the *Irish Field* on the counter in Murray's shop and at once realised that working for this newspaper was his real goal.

Valentine admits that he did not even ride a horse at the time but, being born about a mile from Salisbury racecourse, he could not help but be attracted to the excitement of the track. He began to attend every possible race meeting in England and Ireland, thus acquiring a specialist knowledge which would later come in useful. He remembers going to Cheltenham on Gold Cup Day in 1964 and watching Arkle beating Mill House to win the crown on a memorable day. From then onwards this was his main horse, he says, and racing was his main thing!

The Irish Field

In 1965 he secured a position on financial pages of the *Irish Times*, so he could now realise his ambition of living in Ireland. At the *Irish Times* he worked for Hugh O'Neill, whom he describes as a brilliant journalist and teacher. When O'Neill departed, Valentine was promoted to the position of Financial Editor.

Initially, he lived in the gardener's cottage at Castletown House, and later in a flat in one wing of the house itself. Then, on his marriage to his second wife, Waterford-woman Marie Widger, he moved to Dún Laoghaire. Marie comes from a racing family which won the 1895 Grand National with Wild Man From Borneo.

Douglas Gageby, a man whom Valentine describes as outstanding in his profession, was editor of the *Irish Times* in the 1960s. Valentine's ambition was to secure employment with the *Irish Field*, which was owned by the *Irish Times*, and Gageby duly appointed him editor in June 1970. The *Irish Field* was, and is, the only weekly newspaper which dealt with Irish racing and thoroughbred breeding, so it filled an important niche in the industry. In those days the newspaper was somewhat neglected with no financial investment from the parent company. The staff consisted of a caretaker editor, an advertising manager and the reliable Dave Baker who did most of the journalistic work.

Helped by his five years' journalistic experience from the *Irish Times*, Valentine, with a free hand, broadened the coverage and took over the business side. He introduced new writers both at home and internationally, and developed a show jumping section run by Averil Douglas, who successfully built it up from a single column to a wide-reaching coverage. Valentine recalls that in those days all the racing journalists from the main papers would pile into one car and travel together to cover a meeting.

Major Thomas McDowell controlled the *Irish Times* at this time, and thanks to Douglas Gageby, the newspaper dropped its staid Protestant image to become what it is today, says Valentine. He recalls an occasion when a report was written about a point-to-point in Meath, during which a rider had allegedly whipped a horse to such an extent that it collapsed and had to be put down. This rider sued the *Irish Field* for libel and the Major decided to defend the case. To the amazement of everyone, the case was lost. The cost of the case was about £120,000, with the result that the *Irish Field* budget was hit, which meant that Valentine lost that year's bonus. However, he was compensated: "Luckily the very nice managing director gave me a television at Christmas!"

Some major events occurred in the industry from the 1970s onwards. The Royal Dublin Society made the decision to improve its finances through the sale of the land rented by Goffs for its thoroughbred sales. The company, chaired by top businessman Paddy McGrath, had to change location and although in a precarious financial position, decided to move to a virgin site at Kill, County Kildare. The three McGrath brothers, owner Paddy, breeder Joe and trainer Seamus, were then a force to be reckoned with in the horse industry. Joseph McGrath senior had controlled the highly lucrative Irish Hospitals Sweepstakes.

At this time, the Ballsbridge Sales company was established in direct competition with Goffs, which went public to raise the necessary funding for the new complex at Kill. In a minor coup for Valentine, the *Irish Field* secured significant advertising revenue by running the shareholders' prospectus. The newspaper covered the elaborate launch of the new company, and Valentine recalls meeting an old colleague from the *Financial Times* at a lavish dinner in the King Sitric restaurant in Howth on that occasion.

The Turf Club

In Valentine's time, the Turf Club was run on strict, almost military, lines. Men were referred to by their surnames and jockeys were 'mere' riders of horses, he says. The members, many still wearing bowler hats at the races, were pleasant enough to him, due to the influence of the *Irish Field*, he modestly believes. In a move to restrict the Turf Club's power and improve the industry's funding, a new Government-controlled body was set up at the turn of the century. This body is now known as Horse Racing Ireland.

He remembers the changeover as being bitter, with unprecedented scenes of hundreds of owners, trainers, jockeys, stable lads and others marching to the Turf Club at the Curragh, and handing over a letter demanding that it cede power to the new body. The Turf Club was forced to drop its 'port and stilton' image, and more businessmen were subsequently elected to the Club. He also recalls Minister for Finance Charlie McCreevy saying, "If you join us, we will join you". Nowadays, although the Turf Club retains responsibility for the integrity of racing, it is Horse Racing Ireland which controls the horse industry in this country.

Success stories

A success story covered by the *Irish Field* was the continuing rise of Vincent O'Brien's Ballydoyle Stables and the emergence of Coolmore Stud as the world's most powerful breeding empire. When Valentine began his career with the newspaper, O'Brien had already won three consecutive Grand Nationals and went on to land the Epsom Derby six times. The main driving force today is John Magnier of Coolmore Stud, a man who is single-minded in his ambition to excel in the business, says Valentine. His talent lies in his ability to select the yearlings that will become Classic-winning racehorses and then leading stallions. From his late champion sire Sadler's Wells and Arc de Triomphe-winning mare Urban Sea came Galileo, who won the Epsom Derby. Ballydoyle, now run by Aidan O'Brien, is the premier trainer in both Ireland and England, winning four out of the five English Classics in 2012. Aidan's young son Joe is leading Irish Flat jockey at the tender age of 19.

The financial rescue and development of Punchestown into a modern racecourse was an event which caused major controversy, Valentine recalls. With significant financial help from Horse Racing Ireland it is now successfully run. He remembers the initial divided and bitter feelings among its owners the Kildare Hunt Club, but it all worked out eventually for the good of Irish racing.

The National Stud

Valentine describes the Irish National Stud as a great credit to Irish breeding. In 1915, the stud was gifted to the Crown by Colonel William Hall Walker, a most successful breeder, one of whose endearing innovations was to install skylights in the stables so that the stallions could view the

> " Luckily, the very nice managing director gave me a television at Christmas. "

night sky and thus their breeding prowess could possibly be influenced by the stars! Its present title was incorporated in 1945, and the Stud, Japanese Gardens and Horse Museum are open to the public. Valentine credits former manager Michael Osborne with its great success. The National Stud is a semi-state company, originally intended for the purpose of assisting the small breeder, with fees for stallions being kept as low as possible. It has become more commercial nowadays and a stallion called Invincible Spirit is one of the top 10 sires in Europe, whose fee is €60,000 per cover, and rising.

Today, every race is televised which has naturally had an effect on attendances at race meetings. As Valentine points out, technology brings change, but he believes that it is still vital that journalists cover the stories both on and off the track for print and other media. In his opinion, racing desperately needs to be promoted so that people are attracted back to what can be a most enjoyable day at the races. ■

H. E. President Mary Robinson presenting the Racing Club of Ireland trophy to Valentine Lamb in recognition of The *Irish Field's* essential place within the racing and breeding industry. *Photograph SKP & Associates.*

An Aintree trio on Grand National day. Walter Greacen (left), Leopardstown Tours; Frank Tully, Tully Travel; with Valentine Lamb, looking for the big race winner.

Valentine Lamb (right) drawing a ticket in a nationwide sweepstake involving thousands of shopowners and managers.

Valentine Lamb making a presentation to Charlie Swan. *The Irish Field. Photograph Peter Mooney.*

Dermot Weld's last ride was on winner Midsummer Gamble at Leopardstown on December 27 1986, being led by his son Mark.

CHAPTER 24

DERMOT WELD

" The Twomilehouse Parish Committee decided to find the Irish solution to the Irish problem, which was to buy a racehorse. **"**

PROFILE

Dermot Weld

Rosewell House
The Curragh
Co. Kildare

Born:
1948

Occupation:
Trainer

D ermot Weld, son of Charles and Marguerite Weld, was brought up at Rosewell House on the Curragh. He attended Newbridge College, first as a day student and later as a boarder. He enjoyed his time there and had some great days playing schools rugby. In his spare time he rode and exercised horses. Following matriculation, he attended University College Dublin where he studied veterinary science.

His parents trained racehorses very successfully over many years. Charles Weld, his father, was a trainer who did extremely well with over 1,000 winners. He trained two Champion two-year olds, including Right Strath that won the Phoenix Stakes at the Phoenix Park racecourse in 1963, and Decies, that won the Irish National Stakes at the Curragh in 1969. In addition, there were several National Hunt winners, including the Galway Plate with Highfield Lad in 1959, and Coniston, the winner of two big novice chases at the Gold Cup at Fairyhouse and the Punchestown Gold Cup, both in 1962, with jockey Joe Malone. Dermot remembers Joe as a "main man" in his father's operation. Charlie Weld had the first Irish runner in the Washington DC International Stakes with Farney Fox in 1963, which had been brought over from Ireland with Joe Malone. Joe also worked for Dermot, who describes him as a lynchpin in his own success as a trainer.

Farming was in the blood on both sides of Dermot's family, and both families had kept point to point horses. His mother, Marguerite, from Rathcormack, County Waterford, was a very good point to point rider who had many winners. His father Charlie was from near Naas, and his family also had a tradition of National Hunt horses. Dermot was brought up with horses from a very young age, and he acknowledges his parents as his prime mentors in his successful career.

Dermot is married to Mary, and they have two sons, Mark and Chris, and they also have grandchildren. Both sons are involved with their father in the industry. Horse training is a full-time job Dermot explains, and he very much enjoys it though he also has interests in other sports, such as rugby, which he played at Newbridge College and UCD. He has a seat in the Aviva Stadium in Dublin, and he avidly follows Kildare GAA. He also follows football, and Sir Alex Ferguson, manager of Manchester United, is a good friend who wrote the foreword to his book *Vintage Crop: Against all Odds*, published by Gill and Macmillan in 2009. Dermot enjoys writing, and he hopes to write another book in the future. He remarks that he would like to write about his riding and training career, and perhaps also about training the racehorse.

Amateur jockey

Dermot's amateur career as a jockey began when he finished fourth on Wise Knight at Ballinrobe in 1964, when he was 15 years of age. Not long afterwards, he rode in the Amateurs Derby, a big amateur race at Galway. Ticonderoga was due to be ridden by Tony Cameron who was a leading rider at the time. However, as Dermot recalls, Tony wanted to ride Extra Stout for Dick Hoy in the same race, so Dermot asked his father for the ride. Charlie Weld contacted owner Colonel Reed, in Scarsdale, New York, who agreed to let a 15-year old ride the second race of his life. In a wonderful display, Dermot went on to win the race the day before he turned 16. He recalls that Kevin Prendergast and Bunny Cox, two of the top amateur jockeys at the time, finished second and third. Thus began Dermot's long and successful relationship with the Galway festival.

Dermot explains that riding came very naturally to him, and that he is comfortable and confident on the back of a horse. As he is tall in stature, he had to carefully watch his weight. He says that riding a horse is a very specialised skill which you enjoy or you do not.

Following his successes in his mid teens, he rode in many races, over the following ten to twelve years, and was the leading amateur rider of Ireland on three occasions. Apart from riding winners in Ireland, he has won amateur races all over the world. He won the feature amateur race in France, the biggest amateur race in America (in South Carolina), and, when working as a vet in Pietermaritzburg, South Africa, he was the winner of a hurdle race on Poplin in a professional race. Dermot freely acknowledges that he was fortunate in his rides. The horse picked for him in South Africa went lame and was a non-runner, and the horse he rode was an outside chance to win. Recently when he was looking back at his records, he realised that he had won one out of every three races in which he rode. In one week, he remembers, he rode five wins in five races.

Before he began his studies at University College Dublin, Dermot went to work with American veterinarian, William O'Reid, a position which provided him with great experience. He worked in the back stretch of Belmont Park, the Aqueduct and Saratoga. In the mornings he recalls doing track work in Belmont Park, and then working for the vet for the rest of the day. This experience gave him a good understanding of American racing which would be useful in his later career.

He qualified as a veterinary surgeon at the very young age of 21, and it was said that at that point he was the youngest vet in the world. He is rightly very proud of his achievement. After he qualified, he went to work in Natal for a period in order to gain experience, and it was during this time that he rode to win the big South African race.

Beginning his career as a trainer

When Dermot was 23, his father Charlie Weld retired and became his son's assistant in the business. Though huge responsibility fell on Dermot's young shoulders, he was very fortunate that his parents were there to provide help and guidance. Dermot considers that his father was a better trainer than he. He acknowledges that Charlie was a wonderful father, and that he was also very fortunate to have a great mother who was deeply involved with horses. His mother, Marguerite, is one of the great horse breeders, he says, and he names Grey Swallow, a Derby winner, and Nightime, the winner of the Irish 1,000 Guineas a few years ago. These were just two of the outstanding classic winners which she bred from a small number of mares. Tragically, in what was an enormous shock to the family, Charlie Weld collapsed and died very suddenly at his home at Piper's Hill Stud.

Dermot reflects that Irish racing has stood the test of time. In the 1970s it was going through a difficult patch, but in his first year as trainer, he had 81 winners from a good team of horses. He says that the secret of his success is hard work, knowing the horses, having the right staff, having the ability to delegate and, very importantly, having the ability to place horses where they are most likely to win. A good trainer knows that horses have different levels and abilities. Horses run different distances, and a trainer must know which distance suits a horse.

Nowadays, most horses at Rosewell are owned by international owners, including members of the Makhtoum family who, Dermot says, are good supporters of Rosewell and great supporters of Ireland. Other owners are Prince Khalid Abdullah of Saudi Arabia and Walter Haefner of Moyglare Stud who died in 2012, aged 101. Dermot remarks that he and Mr Haefner had a lot of success together. Other international owners come from the USA, Australia, Japan, China, Italy, France and the UK. Some of his Irish owners include Michael Smurfit and Sir Anthony O'Reilly, along with two former Presidents of Ireland: Mary Robinson and Mary McAleese, whom Dermot describes as "ambassadors for our country". Mary Robinson, he says, is very interested in her horses, which included Moy Water, a winner at Gowran Park. For Mary McAleese, he trained Cairdeas, which was a group winner at the Curragh and was later sold abroad as a stallion.

Teach Dhá Mhíle

With regard to syndicates, Dermot says that during the Celtic Tiger years he trained horses for some syndicates of owners, but he does not have as many as some other trainers. With a smile, he says that dealing with one or two owners at a time is hard enough! However, he tells an entertaining story about one particular syndicated horse Teach Dhá Mhíle, which was owned by the parish of Twomilehouse in County Kildare. This is a small parish between Naas and Kilcullen, and the parish priest at the time, Fr O'Byrne, was a friend of Charlie and Marguerite Weld. The parish was fundraising to renovate the church, though not very successfully. As Dermot says, the committee decided to find the Irish solution to the Irish problem, which was to buy a racehorse. Dermot was given the job of buying the horse, so off he went to Goff's sales. On the last day of the sale he bought a yearling for £7,200 from Martin McHenry, who had bred Red Rum, amongst others. The committee then began selling raffle tickets, with the horse as the prize. In the meantime Dermot was working the horse, and word spread that the horse was good. The raffle took place at Punchestown in late Spring, by which time about £40,000 had

> **“** I started training at the age of 23 and my father was a wonderful assistant to me. **”**

been raised. The next idea was that the winner of the horse, who happened to be a gentleman from Newbridge, might be persuaded to take cash as the prize instead of the horse. Committee member and local Garda detective Jim Heffernan had the job of persuading the winner that it would be a wiser choice to take the money, rather than take on the risks and expense of owning a racehorse. As Dermot says now, the winner wisely decided to take the cash, as one never knows with a horse.

So, Teach Dhá Mhíle now belonged to the Twomilehouse parish fund, and from now onwards, all rewards would go towards the fund. The horse was run in the racing colours of a local farmer, Seán Fitzsimons, which were the colours of the Twomilehouse GAA football club, with Michael Kinane as jockey. Teach Dhá Mhíle won its first race in Killarney in July 1989, it won the Sportsman Challenge race in the Phoenix Park (prize money about £25,000), and it won in a group race at the Curragh. As Dermot tells it, at about a furlong to go at the Curragh, the jockey and horse were faced with a wall, but then with about 100 yards to run a gap appeared, the horse surged forward and duly won the race, which was worth about £30,000 to the winner. At this stage Teach Dhá Mhíle was one of the best two-year olds in Ireland, and there was a lot of interest in buying the horse. Dermot received an offer through the bloodstock agent, Peter Wragg, of about £110,000, but the next job was to persuade the committee to take the money. Fr O'Byrne asked Dermot to talk to the committee to make a case for selling the horse. The committee decided to sell, and Teach Dhá Mhíle went to Italy where it won a group race for its new owners. Back at Twomilehouse the money was well invested, and in 2011 the church was completely renovated.

This is a typically Irish racing story, Dermot remarks. The parish fundraisers had luck on their side: having Dermot to buy the horse, Michael Kinane to ride it and Peter Wragg to buy it. Horse racing is the sport of everybody, whether rich or poor, famous or ordinary. It crosses all divides, he says.

Dermot Weld, who rode and trained Spanner to win the Player-Wills Amateur race at the Galway festival in 1972, 1973 and 1975. Spanner was owned by Mrs N. T. Jackson. Also in the picture are his parents, Charlie (left) and Marguerite.

Ticonderoga winning the 1964 Galway Players Amateur Handicap with 16 year-old Dermot Weld on board.

Dermot Weld, age 21, receiving his degree from UCD.

Dermot with Queen Elizabeth II. *Photograph Caroline Norris.*

Owners and trainers

Dermot and his mother Marguerite own about six horses together, and he has shares in perhaps another half-dozen international horses. Dermot is not a gambling man, he says, at least not at the bookie's! He only bets on his own horses occasionally, and even then he would only back one of them based on his own judgment. As a trainer he is well aware that anything can happen on the day of the race, and that nothing is certain. With regard to training horses, he says that he had to learn to have confidence in his own ability, but importantly, he learnt also to be very careful. A trainer must have excellent staff who will take optimum and proper care of the horses in the yard. Dermot notes that most of his staff have been with him for many years, and he is happy to run the operation as a team. He advises that the breeding of a horse will have a bearing on how it is trained, and pedigree will guide a trainer in which direction to go.

The naming of the horse is the prerogative of the owner, and the name is registered with the Turf Club. The colours the jockey wears are the owner's colours, and the trainer has no involvement in this.

International wins

When asked about the real highlight of his career, Dermot finds it impossible to choose from all the winning horses over the years. As he points out, they all had their own characteristics, and they were all special to him.

Vintage Crop is naturally very special as his first winner of the Melbourne Cup, as is Go and Go, winner of the Belmont Stakes at Belmont Park in Elmont, New York. At that time, it was unheard of for an Irish horse to win the Belmont Stakes. The horse was flown in direct five days before the race. He remembers that it was thought that an Irish-trained horse could not win on a dirt track, but Go and Go disproved this theory when it ran and won with Michael Kinane on board in 1990. He was the seventh fastest ever and, in addition, he beat the winner of the Kentucky Derby. Dermot explains that he does not train a horse differently for dirt or turf. However, he did know Belmont well as he had been there as a young man assisting an American veterinarian. He remains the only non-American to have trained the winner of a leg of the American Triple Crown. This is an achievement in which he takes a quiet pride, and one that he regards as his very best.

When the stable won in Hong Kong with the first ever international horses to run there, Dermot remembers the great reception afforded to them there. He was there in the early days in Dubai, and he recalls a couple of nice winners there. Also notable were wins on the west and east coasts and midwest of the United States of America, and in Australia, South Africa and in all the classic races in Europe. There is no doubt that Dermot Weld is a pioneer in the internationalisation of horse racing worldwide, and he feels that perhaps this is the legacy he will leave when he retires.

Dermot is mainly a Flat race trainer, but he has been fortunate to win every National Hunt race including the Irish Grand National, four Galway plates, three Galway hurdles and every other chase and hurdle race worth winning, including the Irish champion hurdle, the Kerry National and the main races at Leopardstown at Christmas.

On August 7 2000 Dermot Weld surpassed the record for the greatest number of winners, and in April 2011 he trained his 3,500th winner – a horse called Notable Graduate, the winner at Tipperary. He says that he has had nearly 100 winners since then. His trophy room is full of photographs, awards and other memorabilia recording his successes over the years. He has trained the winners for all the Classic races. The list seems to be endless, and includes two Melbourne Cups: Vintage Crop in 1993 and Media Puzzle in 2002.

Wins in the United States of America include Pine Dance, a joint English and American-owned horse, that ran on turf in 2000 in the American Derby Grade 2 Stakes at Arlington Park, Chicago. In 2000 it won the Pennsylvania Derby at Philadelphia Park, and in 2001 it won the Brandywine Stakes at Delaware Park. Dermot won the American Derby at Arlington Park again in 2003 with Evolving Tactics and, for a third time, in 2004 with Simple Exchange. Weld won the Flower Bowl Invitational Stakes, a Grade 1 race, in Belmont Park with Dimitrova in 2004 and the Secretariat Stakes at Arlington Park with Winchester in 2008. He has also been successful in the Matriarch Stakes (Grade 1) at Hollywood Park, Inglewood, and other stakes races around California.

Some of the races in the USA are run on the dirt, and some on a turf that is very firm compared to that in Ireland, though Dermot says that the training is much the same. He was winning Grade 1 races in America before most people were bringing horses from Europe, and now everybody goes there. He likes to think he was a pioneer, he smiles.

As Dermot recalls, people did not travel horses much when he began to do it in the 1980s. His first Grade 1 win in America was at Laurel Park in Maryland in the Laurel Futurity Stakes with Go and Go in 1989. Vintage Crop won the Melbourne Cup in 1993. As Dermot says it was not possible to travel prior to then because of quarantine regulations, and charter flights were not so easy to arrange. In addition, as has already been pointed out, it was felt that horses would not run successfully on the dirt.

Australia has a special place in Dermot's heart. When a young vet, he worked in Sydney, Melbourne and Wagga Wagga, New South Wales, and he nursed a dream of returning there. The first non-Australian horses to race there were Vintage Crop, which he trained and an English horse, Drumtaps. Following his first attempt to win the Melbourne Cup, he was honoured with the freedom of the city of Melbourne, and granted the key to the city. He has also been included in a parade down the city's Collins Street.

The story of winning the Melbourne Cup has now been made into a feature film, with Irish actor Brendan Gleeson taking the part of Dermot Weld in *The Cup* (2011).

Dermot may also be termed a racing pioneer in the Far East, having brought two horses, Additional Risk, owned by Moyglare Stud Farm, and Prudden Manor to Hong Kong for the two big international races held there. Additional Risk ridden by Michael Kinane won the Hong Kong Mile in 1991 with Prudden Manor coming second.

In Italy, Weld trained the Moyglare Stud-owned Again Tomorrow to win the Premio Parioli (the Italian 2,000 Guineas), then a Group 1 race at Capannelle in Rome, in the 1985 Italian Derby.

He has also had many wins on English racetracks, including the Epsom Oaks, the 2,000 Guineas at Newmarket, and a number of big handicaps including the Cesarewitch, seventeen Royal Ascot winners including the Gold Cup in 2010 with Rite of Passage, of which he was part owner. It was very special indeed to win the Ascot Gold Cup. Some of his early wins include the Cheveley Park Stakes at Newmarket with Sookera, owned by Robert Sangster, in 1977, and the Epsom Oaks with Blue Wind, which was his first Classic winner.

In France, champion sprinter fillies like Committed won the Prix de l'Abbaye de Longchamps for two years running in 1984 and 1985. Vinnie Roe won the Prix Royal-Oak in 2001, and there were many other winners.

In a truly remarkable achievement, Dermot Weld won his 3,000th winner abroad in 2005 with King Jock at the Dubai Racing Club.

Winning at home

Dermot Weld has also been a consistent winner at home in Ireland. He recalls some tough horses such as Vinnie Roe, the winner of four consecutive Irish St Legers (2001, 2002, 2003, 2004) and the horse was unlucky not to win a Melbourne Cup as well. A horse bred by his mother Marguerite was Grey Swallow, the winner of the Irish Derby in 2004. In addition, Dermot has been five times winner of the Irish National Stakes, with Diamonds Are Trumps (1977), Day Is Done (1981), Definite Article (1994), Mus-If (1998), and Refuse to Bend (2002). With Flash of Steel, owned by Bertram Firestone and ridden by Michael Kinane, he won the Irish 2,000 Guineas at the Curragh in 1986.

All of Dermot Weld's achievements are important to him, and he feels that he has been very fortunate in his life and is very much appreciative of any awards that he has received. Being honoured as Freeman of city of Melbourne is very special to him as a non-Australian. He also feels very honoured to have been awarded the Charter Day medal from UCD in 2001, awarded in acknowledgment of his international success as a racehorse trainer, for work done on the development council of UCD, and for his involvement as chairman in bringing the veterinary college from Shelbourne Road to its new location in Belfield.

The veterinary school at UCD is naturally close to Dermot's heart as this is where he trained as a young vet. In 2000 the school was one hundred years old, and despite great efforts, the money for a new building could not be raised. When requested, Dermot agreed to take on the task of becoming directly involved with the project aimed at moving the school from one site to another. He chaired the committee, but he is quick to acknowledge that other people also worked very hard. He had the contacts, he says, but there were others doing the work. He made business submissions to Charlie McCreevy, Minister for Finance at that time, but the crucial issue was that there were four government departments involved: the Department of the Environment owned the property, it was a Department of Agriculture-approved college and the Departments of Finance and Education were also involved. In addition, the committee was fundraising from many sources, and major finance was required.

Eventually it was decided that the existing premises should be sold, as the most money could be raised by this means. Dermot remembers that initially the valuation was about £7 million, but later the property was sold for £28 million. As is generally known, the land was subsequently sold for more than €150 million.

UCD used the £28 million raised to build the new veterinary building at Belfield, and Dermot subsequently presented a monument to be placed there, known as 'The Egg'. Politics did play a part in the proceedings, but Dermot believes that racing is above politics and, in Ireland, he has found the three main political parties very supportive of racing. For example, Charlie McCreevy, former Minister for Finance, Joe Walsh, former Minister for Agriculture and Simon Coveney, present Minister for Agriculture, Food and the Marine are all extremely supportive of racing.

The Galway races are very important to Dermot Weld, and he has been presented with an award for his achievements as a trainer by the Galway Race Committee. He rode his first winner in Galway at 15 years of age, and had his 200th winner there in 2008. He has since been made a member of the committee at Galway. Following a very successful first year as a trainer, bookmaker Seán Graham designed and presented him with the Young Trainer of the Year for Ireland award due to the number of wins he had achieved in his first year. The racecourses at Tralee, Listowel and Killarney were also good for him. Dermot won the Dawn Light Leading Trainer Award, sponsored by Kerrygold, in Kerry in 1987, 1991, 1992, 1993 and 1999. Later, around 2002, in recognition of his achievements as a trainer, and especially his achievement in winning the Melbourne Cup, he received an award, carved from bog oak, from the Stewards of the Turf Club. He has many other awards in his trophy room, including the Canon Hayes National Sports Award 2002.

He is really happy to have received three Texaco Awards for achievements in sport. He was also named Sport Star of the Year on two occasions. Being voted Person of the Year for Ireland in 2002-2003, sponsored by the *Sunday Independent*, is of great importance to Dermot who says he appreciates this probably more than anything. He has been given many awards by the Trainers Association, including a lifetime achievement award, and Kildare County Council made a special presentation to him a couple of years ago. In addition to his many Irish awards, he has also received international awards in England, America and Australia.

The importance of the industry to the economy

Dermot Weld not only trains horses, but he also takes an active part in the industry. He has served on the old Racing Board and later on the Irish Horse racing Authority. He has also been a member of the board of the Irish National Stud. He notes the differing emphases in relation to Horse Racing Ireland and the Turf Club. Horse Racing Ireland is very much involved with finance and the day-to-day running costs of racing, while the Turf Club is in charge of security and integrity.

Horse racing is a major industry that attracts people from all walks of life. Horses are trained in all twenty-six counties in Ireland and there are a lot of valuable spin-offs from the business. Dermot currently employs eighty-three people, and his staff live in the local area with resultant economic benefits. In addition, the yard buys hay and straw from farmers, foodstuff mostly from Red Mills in Kilkenny, and provides employment to farriers, saddlers and others. Like any business, a lot of common sense is always required. Dermot points out that the horse racing industry does not receive major grants from government. He firmly believes that it is a natural industry of our country, and something at which the Irish inherently excel. Ireland has the limestone land, the temperate climate and its people have horsemanship which is admired worldwide. He feels that it is vital that the industry be nurtured, developed and cared for, and he knows that it has a great future.

In all his years, Dermot has found that racing is above politics, and he is adamant that he has not met with any political party that is less than positive in its perception of the industry. Politicians are aware of the employment it provides – currently about 16,000 people are directly employed in the industry. Not only is the thoroughbred horse racing industry a huge employer, it is a great asset to Irish tourism. Dermot concludes that as long as the prize money structure is sufficient to encourage people to have horses in training in Ireland, they will continue to support the industry.

Rosewell House currently has about 100 horses in its yard. Dermot feels himself very fortunate, as most of the owners he has trained for have been with him for many years, including, for example, Bert Firestone who has had horses from America at Rosewell House, and also the late Walter Haefner of Moyglare Stud who was a great patron since the very early days.

Dermot Weld is a most accomplished individual, and a person who has contributed much to the Irish horse racing industry, and to its reputation of excellence in far flung places around the world where the sport of kings is supported and relished. ■

Dermot at Royal Ascot. *Photograph Caroline Norris.*

Michael Kinane after winning on Asema at the Curragh in April 1993. *The Irish Field. Photograph Caroline Norris.*

CHAPTER 25

MICHAEL KINANE

“ It's not a question of how you fall, it's how
you pick yourself up! ”

PROFILE

Michael Kinane

Punchestown
Co. Kildare

Born:
1959

Occupation:
Jockey

Michael Kinane is proud to say that he comes from a family of jockeys. In the previous generation his father Tommy and his uncles Danny, Billy, Christy and Ned were all National Hunt jockeys who started out in Tim Hyde's in Ballinahinch, Co Tipperary. Some of them later went into training. Three of Michael's siblings were also National Hunt jockeys, including his eldest brother Thomas, a very good amateur jockey who rode many winners. His younger brother James rode winners in Ireland and England, and another brother Paul was also very successful. Michael also has three sisters, Susan, Catherine and Jeannette.

Michael (Mick) Kinane grew up in Holy Cross and later at Killenaule, County Tipperary, where his father farmed and trained a few horses. While his parents were keen for their son to get a full education, Mick fell in love with racing at an early age, and education fell by the wayside. During the mid-1970s, while still at school, he would ride out during the school holidays in order to gain experience, and during the Easter holidays in 1975, he signed up to Liam Browne as an apprentice. On a break during his school exams, he got the offer of a ride in an apprentice race from Larry Green. Mick went off to ride Muscari in the 1½ mile race at Leopardstown, which he won in 1975, and he recalls that it was fellow apprentice Tommy Carmody who gave him advice on how to approach the race. The next day he went back to school to finish his exams and he left school at lunch time. That was the end of his formal education because he went riding for Liam Browne for what was intended to be a period of three weeks. Thus his amazingly successful career began at 15 and from this incredible start he has never looked back.

Mick always assumed that he would be a National Hunt jockey as were all his uncles and brothers. His father was anxious that he should start on the Flat to get a "polish", as he thought that Mick would acquire the change of style in riding on the Flat. Mick feels that it was fortunate that he followed his father's advice as it marked the start of a good career, and was also less dangerous. Unlike his brothers, Mick has been fortunate in not becoming too heavy. Over his career, he averaged 8 stone 7 pounds, the maintenance of which did involve some extreme discipline at times, most especially in his twenties.

Apprentice jockey

Mick's apprenticeship began with Liam Browne on the Curragh in March 1976, at various stables including Rathbride and Maddenstown. He recalls the tough work, which included a very early start each day, mucking out and then riding out as many horses as was necessary. There was a break for lunch, and then more riding until about 6 p.m. In his first year he had two winners and a lot of rides, and then in the second year things picked up. As he says himself, if you were fortunate enough to go racing, that gave more of a break to the day. The work continued seven days a week, with about two days off at Christmas, if he was lucky. When he began his apprenticeship at the age of 15, he was placed in digs which were paid for out of his wages, and then he was given about £2 for the week.

Mick declares that it is a desire for horses which drives everything, not the amount of money earned. It is not a 9 to 5 career, he says, and the horses must be looked after. You must have a passion for it, and will never succeed if you come at it from any other direction. He recalls that difficulties can arise in the early days of an apprenticeship as apprentices are launched into an adult world and it is hard for adolescents to stay focussed. It really is important, he emphasises, to have a love for horses.

An enquiry about the identity of his hero in those early days, brings an instant response of "Lester Piggott". Mick got to know his idol quite well over the years, and he respects Lester as, in his opinion, it was he who elevated jockeys from being third-class citizens in the industry to being genuine sportsmen.

Turning professional

After his seven-year apprenticeship, Mick Kinane began his professional career. About two years earlier, Michael Kauntze "put a claim on him" under an agreement with Liam Browne, and thus he began work in Ashbourne Stables for Michael Kauntze. This marked a good progression from apprentice to professional. The stable had a nice clientèle of owners, and he says that Michael Kauntze was a lovely man to work for. Mick's five years there gave him a taste of professionalism. He explains that during this period, everyone is looking at the young jockey to see how he might shape up, and so it can be a slow start to getting good rides. He had been lucky not to have sustained any serious injuries as an apprentice, but during his time with Kauntze he broke his wrist four or five times.

Keeping in shape is very important for a professional jockey. Mick admits to having smoked at one time, but he gave it up as a bad habit. What he terms "race riding fitness" is a specialist type of fitness and it cannot be achieved any other way. Riding full-time, probably eight or ten races a day on four or five days a week, plus travel, will keep you fit. He says that the most boring part of his job was the travel, and that the work only becomes repetitive when one is working with bad horses. However, there is no time to be bored during a race because each race is unique and is run in a highly charged atmosphere, with twenty jockeys, packed tight, going around at forty miles an hour.

Flat races, he says, are safer than National Hunt, and in his opinion, jump jockeys are not paid enough for what they take on. His father, Tommy Kinane, rode in the Grand National, and Mick often wondered what it might be like, but he reached the stage where he did not see the point of taking it on.

He is well aware of how lucky he was to have never broken a leg, and despite other 'normal' injuries, he has had just one bad fall. This was in Hong Kong, riding on the inside at Happy Valley, a tight track. A gap opened up on the rail, he went for it, but as he says the horse was not so brave, and it clipped a heel and flipped over. Mick was out for six weeks. He explains that when a jockey has a bad fall, he is fortunate if he is not conscious. On this occasion, Mick was conscious throughout, which was difficult. He points out there are not too many sports in which you are followed by two ambulances – that is the context of this tough game. Once a jockey becomes afraid of it, he says, it is time to walk away.

Regarding the financial aspect of a jockey's career, Mick explains that there is a fee for riding a horse, then there is a percentage of the prize money, and there may also be retainers. Obviously, there are deductions such as taxes and pension payments. Naturally, the more successful a jockey is, the more he can make. If very successful, a jockey will try to get a retainer from a big yard for whatever he can get. If a jockey is fortunate, then he'll be winning 15-20% of the time. Things will, and do, go wrong at times, and when this happens, a jockey has to pick himself up. "It's not a question of how you fall, it's how you pick yourself up", he says.

The greatest number of rides for Mick in one day was on the occasion when he rode in ten out of the eleven races on the card at the Phoenix Park when he was an apprentice. When in Hong Kong, he often rode ten in a day. He explains that some days are harder than others, but you take what you can. It is particularly difficult if the temperature is high, for instance, in Hong Kong or Dubai, when a jockey can become dehydrated, and although taking on fluid is important, this has weight implications, so it all becomes a balancing act. Jockeys are obsessed about their weight as it is crucial to their work, and each fellow would have his own comfort zone. As already stated, Mick's weight was generally 8 stone 7 pounds, though he could ride at 8 stone 4 pounds if required, but that was a difficult weight for him. Keeping down the weight means discipline, and is quite demanding.

Becoming recognised

In 1982, Liam Browne, his old boss, asked Mick to ride Dara Monarch in the Irish 2,000 Guineas at the Curragh where he was a winner. He rode Dara Monarch again that year to win the St James' Palace Stakes at Royal Ascot. This was Mick's first major breakthrough in his fourth year as a professional, and gave him important exposure in England. At the time, the tendency was for Irish jockeys not to hold on to rides when horses went to races in England where English jockeys were generally used. With a smile, Mick recalls that it was Lester Piggott who rode Dara Monarch the following year – but he did not win!

Other successes followed, such as winning the Prix de l'Abbaye at Longchamp in 1985 on Committed, trained by Dermot Weld, the Golden Jubilee Stakes on Big Shuffle in 1987 and the Irish 1,000 Guineas on Trusted Partner in 1988.

On the subject of any jealousy which may arise among jockeys who travel abroad with horses, Mick says that there are a lot of Irish jockeys over in England who had made their careers there. He himself never found any jealousy amongst the jockeys, and he feels that they respect that you are there for a reason, and the reason is that you are good enough. He admits that, of course, there is competition and rivalry between the jockeys, but they mostly get along because they are in the same circle. A selfish rider gets shown up pretty quickly, as each jockey is responsible for the

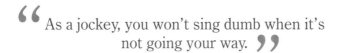

“ As a jockey, you won't sing dumb when it's not going your way. ”

general safety of all. A jockey will not have the respect of fellow professionals if he behaves badly. When a race is being run and a jockey is travelling well, you'll give no quarter, Mick continues. However, when you're not travelling well, you'll give room to someone else. Each jockey only has an instant to react while travelling at forty miles an hour in the middle of a race. The Queen's English is not used out there, and there's lots of shouting and roaring. On a tight track, a jockey cannot go wide, so the pack are tightly bunched. Things happen on a racecourse that will not suit every jockey, and as Michael says, "you won't sing dumb when it's not going your way!"

Returning to his own story, he explains that after spending five years working with Michael Kauntze, he returned to work with Liam Browne for a year. Liam had asked him to return as the stable had been expanded, and Mick went on to have a decent year there. In 1984, he got an offer to ride for Dermot Weld on retainer. This was a big step forward, and there was a good choice of horses with Weld. Mick recalls that initially there was a perception that perhaps he was not the right man for the job, and there was also some jealousy as it was felt that he would never be as good as the current jockeys. However, in 1984, he became Irish Champion Jockey in his first year there. He was now working with Dermot Weld and Walter Haefner of Moyglare Stud, and he says that Haefner was one of his major patrons.

Trainer Dermot Weld with jockey Michael Kinane after Humbel had won at Leopardstown in May 1996.
The Irish Field. Photograph Caroline Norris.

Michael Kinane at an exhibition to celebrate his career at the
Curragh racecourse in 2010. *Photograph Shane O'Neill.*

Michael Kinane with Vincent & Jacqueline O'Brien at the
Celebration of Irish Racing at the Curragh Racecourse on
Ryder Cup Raceday 2008. *Photograph Caroline Norris.*

Michael Kinane in celebratory mood.

He recalls that his relationship with Dermot Weld in the early days was not easy, because Weld is very specific on how a jockey rides, and how he conducts himself in a race. As Mick puts it, maybe his own character did not bend as easily as Weld might have wanted, but now they have ended up with a great relationship. Mick reveals himself as something of a philosopher as he muses that nothing good comes easily or without a lot of hard work.

'A slow horse is still a slow horse'

Mick Kinane says he has been very lucky in his career because he is a very instinctive rider. A jockey can be given orders, but straight out of the stalls the plans might need to change. A jockey never refuses a good start, and a bad start is often very hard to make up. A lot depends on the horse, and the race itself is a balancing act. He stresses that it is very important to know the field, know the track and know the jockeys, and how they might react in various situations during a race.

With regard to horses, he says that sometimes there is marvellous bond. However, it is often better to know nothing about a horse before a race, as he might be a 'nutter' and you might be better not knowing about it, as it could cause apprehension. And can slow horses be made to travel faster? No, laughs Mick, a slow horse is still a slow horse no matter what.

On the question of force he would have imposed on a horse, he says that he only used the whip when necessary, and was never in any trouble with regard to excessive use. He would only whip as a last resort, and a horse can only be coaxed when you are 'tight' with it. As to whether he prefers to be at the front in a race or to come from behind, he says that it is hard to win from the front as you are breaking the ground for everyone else, and it is hard for a horse to stay focussed when out at the front. It is easier to come from not too far off the pace.

Over the years, changing styles of riding have come about, because on television, the movement has to look tidy and be pleasing on the eye. With regard to the change in posture, this has come about mainly due to the introduction of the starting stalls. He explains that the jockey's legs are drawn up to above the maximum width of the horse, because if the horse goes against the side of the metal stall when the gates open, the jockey's body needs to be out of the way as otherwise it will be crushed.

As a professional jockey, Mick used his own saddle and tack. A safety aspect is involved here, as a jockey is only as safe as what he is sitting on while travelling at forty miles per hour around the track. He had four sets of tack: one set in England, one in France and two in Ireland, one of which is for travelling. He liked to use pieces of tack which he thought would suit the horses best.

When the stakes are high, the owners and trainers need confidence that they have the right man on board. It takes a lot of work to gain that confidence, and to gain recognition in that way. Luck is needed to get started, but ability has then to be proven.

Racecourses

A jockey needs to learn about various racecourses in order to get the best out of his horse, Mick continues. He has ridden on all the great tracks in the world, and says that the main tracks are in good shape. However, the country tracks in Ireland are not so good to ride, having a lot of sharp turns and undulating ground with plenty of variety. The jockey's skill is to balance the horse during the race. In reply to a query as to his favourite racecourse, he declares that wherever he was winning was always great!

It is difficult for a jockey not to become involved in the atmosphere at the great racing festivals such as Galway or Punchestown, but he stresses that a jockey cannot really get too involved with the social side of the event as this could be distracting. However, professionally a jockey can add a lot to an event which brings so much to a local area.

International success

The thoroughbred horse racing business has become huge in Ireland, supporting many people. The stakes are high and a horse that wins a classic race suddenly becomes a huge commodity as it can then enhance the breeding. The day-to-day events are very important to the trainer or the owner, and every race, whether at Killarney or Ascot, is important to someone. "A race at Listowel is the Epsom Derby to the owner", Mick says.

The excitement of winning can be incredible for everyone involved, Mick continues. However, if expectations are not too high, a win is truly fantastic. If the win is expected by everyone, his reaction to a win would be one of almost relief, as anything other than a win would have been a disappointment. As a professional, he got more enjoyment from a win if there was no pressure. One thing he consistently finds amazing is that whether the owner is a grocer or a multi-millionaire, the reaction to winning is the same. Watching the owner's reaction is a fantastic and hugely emotional experience, he says.

A jockey has a huge responsibility to perform to his best. However, like any sportsman, a jockey is only as good as his last performance. When a jockey is winning all the time he can command more money. As progress is made, the jockey is in demand by the bigger stables, which is the goal of every jockey. As to the size of the fee that the jockey receives, this is reflected in who wants a jockey the most.

Dermot Weld was Mick Kinane's boss for quite a long time. He was retained to Dermot, so that he had first call on him for his services. Later, Mick was on a second retainer from His Highness the Aga Khan for a spell, and then from Sheikh Mohammed; he wanted to be involved wherever the Group 1 races were run. These arrangements gave him flexibility, and they suited Dermot Weld also. When a jockey becomes successful, the major players will come looking for him. While successful at home and in England, Mick credits the beginnings of his international career to his successes in Italy. At that time, there was no Sunday racing in Ireland, so every Sunday he went to Italy to race and he gradually picked off various wins, including a guineas race for Dermot Weld. Then he won the Prix de l'Arc de Triomphe on

Carroll House in 1989 for the first time, and there followed a very successful period in his career which placed him firmly on the international stage.

He is the only non-American jockey to win the Belmont Stakes. This happened in 1990 when he was aboard Go and Go, also non-American. Go and Go was owned and bred by Walter Haefner at Moyglare Stud, and trained by Dermot Weld. The horse had won the important Laurel Futurity at Laurel Park in Maryland in 1989, and he was placed in the Belmont Stakes at Belmont Park in New York, the longest race of the US Triple Crown series at 1½ miles. As Mick says, it is perceived that riding on dirt is faster, but he does not agree with this perception. The biggest factor for the horse is the kickback from the track. Once a horse handles that, all is well. This win by Go and Go was a huge international achievement for all parties involved, as this American Classic had not and has not since been won by a non-American horse and jockey. After the race in 1990, Go and Go was put in for Saratoga, but now Mick Kinane was a marked man and was, he says, taken out at the start and did not get the same chance. He recalls that the horse got a terrible fright, and was never the same afterwards. The thoroughbred horse is fragile, and it is hard to keep him in top form.

There were some great successes in England also, including his first Derby at Epsom in 1993 on Commander in Chief. This was a second string horse owned by Khalid Abdullah and trained by Henry Cecil. In that race, Pat Eddery rode the favourite Tenby, but it was an easy win for Mick and it proved a big turning point in his career.

His next move was to the stables of Aidan O'Brien at Ballydoyle. O'Brien was then becoming a huge power, and this period proved the most satisfying of Mick Kinane's career. In six years, he had 57 Group 1 winners, including Galileo, son of Sadler's Wells, which he describes as a very special horse. Galileo won the Epsom Derby in 2001, and also won the Irish Derby and the King George VI Stakes in the same year.

Mick Kinane believes that Aidan O'Brien is a great trainer. He can be very intense, he says, but as a top trainer, he has to be demanding of others. While Mick worked at Ballydoyle, O'Brien would sometimes tell him how to ride, at other times he was allowed to use his own discretion.

Sea The Stars

Mick's favourite horse of all time was Sea The Stars, owned by Christopher Tsui and trained by John Oxx. He spent a lot of time with this extraordinary animal, and he says that he was one of the few he got very close to. His dam was Urban Sea which Michael had ridden in a German guineas race years before. Other horses out of Urban Sea which he rode were Galileo and Black Sam Bellamy (Tattersalls Gold Cup in 2003). He believes that Sea The Stars could have done anything because he was such an exceptional horse, and he proved to be very important in the two last years of Mick's career. When Mick retired in 2009 he had reached the age of fifty. Although he feels there is no substitute for experience on a big day, youth and enthusiasm are also factors. At the end, he still had the nerve, he says, but felt it was time to walk away while still on top. Sea The Stars had won six Grade 1 races, and he did not see another horse around that he could continue with at such a high level. It is not often in sport that you can choose when to finish, and Mick Kinane chose to finish on a high.

Life away from horses

Working in the garden or on the farm today is a real joy, and he finds manual labour very therapeutic. When he retired he had a yard on the Curragh, but he decided that he did not want to train. For the past twelve years he has lived with his wife Helen near Punchestown racecourse.

Kildare-woman Catherine Helen Clark and Mick Kinane married in 1983, and they have travelled all over the world together.

Mick feels privileged that opportunities came his way in life, and he knows that he is one of the few who got to ride more than his fair share of good horses. As a child, all he ever wanted to be was a jockey, so he says that he has lived the dream. His final message to jockeys, and perhaps to all of us, is that it is great to soak up the atmosphere at race meetings, but one must not be distracted. It is crucial to focus when leaving the gates. The philosopher emerges once again, as Mick gives this counsel to young jockeys, "The loudest thing you must hear are your own thoughts"; and "Be in the moment, it is a great place to be in and a great place to go." ■

Trainer Dermot Weld with jockey Michael Kinane.